Conflict Fluent

Mastering the Five Conflict Approaches

Emily Taylor

Mediator, Conflict Coach, and Mother of Five

Collaborative Book Works
EVERYDAY CONFLICT RESOLUTION

Collaborative Book Works is an imprint of
Em Taylor Communications, LLC.
126 W. 3960 N.
Provo, UT 84604
www.collaborativebookworks.com

Edited by Shelley Sperry of Sperry Editorial and Erika Magaoay
Cover Image and Book Formatting by Nada Orlic of Erelis Design
Author Photo by Kaitlyn McEntire Photography

Library of Congress Control Number: 2021914640

Publisher's Cataloging-in-Publication data

Names: Taylor, Emily de Schweinitz, author.
Title: Conflict fluent: mastering the five conflict approaches / Emily de Schweinitz Taylor.
Description: Includes bibliographical references. | Collaborative Books Works, 2021.
Identifiers: LCCN: 2021914640 | ISBN: 978-0-9991717-2-1 (paperback) | 978-0-9991717-3-8 (ebook)
Subjects: LCSH Conflict management. | Interpersonal relations. | Interpersonal communications. | Self actualization (Psychology). | Self help. | BISAC FAMILY & RELATIONSHIPS / Conflict Resolution | SELF-HELP / Communication & Social Skills | SELF-HELP / General
Classification: LCC HM1126 .T39 2021 | DDC 305.235--dc23

To my husband, Ken, who has taught me the most about becoming a real-life peacemaker. Thank you for providing the love and security for me to discover what it really means to make peace one day at a time. I look forward to our days ahead with ever-increasing opportunities to love and care for each other.

CONTENTS

Preface

One morning at work, I receive a call from Thomas who is desperate to save his marriage. Agonized and distraught, Thomas shares that his wife, Sherry, is ready to divorce him. He's tried over and over to convince her not to leave, but she's determined and unwilling to talk with him or meet with yet another marriage counselor. Following the last counselor's recommendation to try mediation, Thomas is making a last-ditch effort to connect with his wife.

After talking with Thomas, I reach out to Sherry to gauge her interest in mediating with her estranged husband. When I begin explaining that mediation is like a guided negotiation, she becomes quiet and suggests that it might not be worth it because she's already set on divorce. I explain that I have no set agenda for her marriage, that she is just coming to mediation to talk, and that any agreement she and Thomas reach may be reviewed by an attorney. Upon hearing this, she decides to try what I'm suggesting.

As I hang up the phone, my heart starts beating a little faster. I contrast my office's more mundane mediation cases about security deposit returns and roommate conflicts with Thomas and Sherry's high stakes marital conflict. After countless marriage counseling sessions, will my attempt to help this couple collaborate in mediation make a difference?

As a mediator and conflict resolution coach, I've watched from the front lines as divisions have grown wider and deeper in the United States, in our local communities, and even in our families over the past few years. More and more people have approached me with questions about personal and political conflicts, and I've learned from each new question and situation.

If we're honest, most of us feel threatened and confused by the polarization we see around us, which can lead to paralysis and despair. I've certainly felt that myself at times, but during more than a decade in the field of conflict resolution, I've learned that *choosing action and hope is always better than choosing paralysis and despair.*

All of us can learn how to make peace with ourselves and with each other by developing new skills and fresh approaches to conflict. We can expand how we perceive and interact with each other in conflicts of all kinds. I've written this book because I believe wholeheartedly in our individual capacities to overcome ineffective patterns and develop new, more effective ones.

I've been on my own peacemaking journey, much of which I'll share with you in the chapters that follow. I hope you will open your heart and mind to the possibility of joining me to become a peacemaker too. You'll gain the skills and knowledge to effectively meet the conflicts you face every day, and I think you'll find, as I did, that the journey will reveal new vistas, greater connection with others, and acceptance of yourself and your own deepest needs.

A New Path to Kindness through Conflict

I was a little girl who threw her bicycle helmet in the bushes on the way to school to avoid being teased, climbed onto the fridge late at night to sneak into Grandpa's chocolates without permission, and anxiously hid in my room when a family member got angry. I avoided conflict instead of dealing with it directly.

I'm sure all those strategies are familiar to you. They're fine ways of coping for a six or seven-year-old, but less helpful—and often dangerous—when we get older.

When we take the time to reflect on the way we behave in conflicts, we can feel trapped—like our actions are determined by in-born, unchanging personality traits. But our approaches to conflict are really more about choices we've made and patterns we've learned through thousands of lived experiences at home, at school, and in our communities. If we pause to take a clear-eyed look at ourselves, we can see that while some of our choices and patterns around conflict have served us well over the years, others have crippled us, making it harder to find the love, belonging, and connection we crave.

In my life as a conflict avoider, I usually chose to smooth over, fix, or prevent friction. My misguided idea of kindness included acts like giving up my place in line, staying silent when others insulted me, or not telling my roommate that I had a crush on the guy she liked. Rather than directly facing conflict, I accommodated others, assuming that was the best strategy for happiness. This sometimes helped me escape heartache, but not always.

Too often, in my twenties and thirties, I assumed others would somehow *guess* what I needed and fulfill my wishes without my spelling them out. By trying to circumvent conflict and avoid coming across as needy, I missed out on the intimacy that happens when we constructively deal with conflict.

And intimacy, more than anything else, brings us real happiness.

Finally, in my forties, a little light turned on in my mind, illuminating some important questions I needed to ask myself about the conflicts in my life. I decided to make serious changes to create deeper, truer connections with others, especially those I disagreed with.

Kindness, I realized, had to become more than just sucking it up and sacrificing in every version of conflict.

Sacrifice is often part of kindness, of course, but my version had become more of a weakness than a strength. True kindness isn't just about making sure everyone else gets what they want; being kind includes being *direct, assertive, firm,* and *collaborative* with people in order to meet our own personal needs, too.

My transformation kickstarted with formal conflict resolution training in graduate school. As I participated in courses in negotiation, persuasion, facilitation, and conflict theory, I began rewriting my beliefs, attitudes, and behaviors. I started trying out new ways of facing differences in my personal life. I learned I was not alone in relying on avoidance and accommodation to get through conflict, and I realized that others had often competed with me and gotten their way because I didn't advocate strongly enough for my needs.

Despite the power of these insights, I felt despair when I realized how much I had missed out on in my earlier life. Rather than letting people know the real me, including all of my idiosyncrasies and vulnerabilities, I had regularly presented a version of myself willing to do whatever was needed to make others happy. I hid behind a wall I created between the real me and the image I thought others wanted to see. I now knew that to constructively deal with conflict I had to learn to be open and vulnerable enough to talk directly with others about hard problems—even if they disagreed with me.

Before that turning point, I had rarely been willing to face conflict in a direct and vulnerable way, and I realized that had made me sad for a long time.

After processing my grief about what could have been if I'd known how to handle conflict better earlier, I began learning to expand my conflict toolkit, unlearning old habits I had developed to protect myself from others' moods and demands. I also began to learn how to advocate for myself using alternative approaches. As my confidence grew, I knew I wanted to share what I'd learned with others so they could avoid the same kind of regrets I'd experienced and live more meaningful lives.

That's what this book is all about.

Why "Conflict Fluent?"

Early in my graduate studies, I learned about Five Conflict Approaches used by theorists Kenneth W. Thomas and Ralph H. Kilmann, who developed a personal conflict assessment tool in the 1970s.[1] After taking their conflict styles assessment, I began to better understand my own conflict resolution patterns and how those worked in my relationships with others. Soon, another light went on in my mind, and I realized that a fully developed person should know how to apply each of the Five Conflict Approaches. We all need to master those approaches and be able to deploy them in the right contexts if we want to fulfill personal goals, build relationships, and experience peace.

I started to envision how I could master the Five Conflict Approaches, learning to connect with people on much deeper levels while maintaining my own self-respect and dignity.

I soon felt something revolutionary happening in my life.

Building upon my personal epiphany, I began keeping notes and developing my ideas. Eventually, I had the outline of a book.

As my ideas kept evolving and expanding, I began searching for a title for my project, and I found inspiration in Gary Chapman's popular book, *The Five Love Languages*.[2] Chapman describes the importance of learning another's preferred love language and using that love language when interacting with them.

But in this book, I recommend becoming "fluent" in *all* of the five basic conflict resolution approaches so you can flexibly address different types of conflict as they arise. Let's be honest—we'll all face *multiple* conflicts within every relationship—it's inevitable! And you need the right approach, or language, for each. I ultimately decided to call my book *Conflict Fluent* and my approach, "conflict fluency," based on ideas I first encountered in an influential book I read in graduate school about managing intercultural conflict.[3]

One last note about the concept of fluency: When you become fluent in a foreign language, you don't always say the right thing, despite your technical skills. Fluency takes practice in a variety of social situations. Fluency means you have access to the vocabulary, grammar, accent, and other aspects of a language, but not necessarily the ability to perfectly apply everything you know to achieve seamless human communication.

When you become fluent in the five approaches I talk about in this book, you will have a new set of tools—but it will take time and life experiences to be able to apply each approach in a variety of situations to resolve conflicts successfully. It's a long-term goal, but I can tell you that it's incredibly worthwhile.

Getting Personal

Whenever you write about your personal failures and triumphs, you risk offending others and sharing details that may feel too personal. In writing this book, I hesitated to use examples from my own life at first, but eventually realized that I wanted to share from my heart. So, in this book, I share my motivations, failures, and fears. I expose some of my roughest edges and vulnerabilities. When I'm writing about friends, colleagues, and family, however, I often change names and details to protect their privacy.

By being honest, I hope to show you our common humanity. I also hope I can help you avoid unnecessary suffering. My choices have never been perfect. In many cases, I'll suggest better ways of overcoming conflict and finding personal peace than the paths that I've taken.

Real conflict resolution nearly always involves deeply personal revelations, so I expect you will experience regret, sadness, self-judgment, and more as you read this book and stir up memories. You might be discouraged at first, but you'll soon start to understand your own actions in conflict better. You'll see that you can create more effective patterns to live a more fulfilling, joyful life. I hope that reading this book will be both an emotional and intellectual experience, because we all need both.

The real test of whether or not conflict fluency makes sense for you will come as you put the ideas into practice in real life. Avoiding all conflict by being the perfect kind of person or finding the perfect kind of people to surround yourself with is impossible. Just expect, plan, and prepare for *constructive conflict resolution.*

You'll soon see that you have options in all moments of conflict, whether in your marriage, with your kids, at work, or out in the community. You can actively choose paths that will not only get you where you want to go, but will also help others find greater peace, too.

Conflict is defined most simply as "differences that matter," and I believe we're all different enough to need each other and similar enough to love each other.

Your path to connection with the people you love—and even those you might not love so much right now—requires navigating the differences that matter to get to the intimacy that's vital to live your best life today, tomorrow, and always.

Introduction

One late summer night in 2020, I sat outdoors among a small group of friends chatting and laughing. In the midst of our happy, silly talk, I was caught off guard when my friend Ella asked me an earnest question.

"Emily, how can a conservative vote for someone like that?"

I felt a shift in the mood of the room. Ella's sincere look pushed me to respond even though I usually avoid talking about politics with people I know will disagree with me. I relaxed my boundaries and began sharing personal thoughts that I knew contradicted the opinions of most of the people around me.

Despite the fact that our initial conversation was just between the two of us, others in the group began listening in. They, too, wanted to know what I thought and why.

I looked around and wondered, "Why did I even start down this road? Where is this going to lead?" But I continued.

I tried to focus on Ella, who was listening intently. I cited sources to back up my ideas and saw eyes roll as some of our friends started side conversations refuting what I'd just said.

I knew this was going to happen, I thought, and I started to feel cornered, defensive, and angry. I hated being put on the spot with others judging my information and challenging the views I usually kept private. I wondered what to do next, not wanting to say something I might regret. My relationships with all those people mattered to me, but so did my integrity. Despite my fears, I wanted to be honest, but before I let all my feelings and thoughts loose, I decided to leave the gathering and call it a night.

I left feeling exposed and misunderstood by my friends. No one called me out aggressively, but I felt bathed in disapproval, making me deeply uncomfortable.

Should I have refused to answer Ella and avoided those difficult, divisive topics in "mixed" company? Is complete avoidance in situations like that the best policy? I left the conversation that night gun-shy and wary of sharing from my heart in the future, but I also knew I was giving up something valuable. If I always avoided conflict, I would never create strong and lasting connections with those friends.

I know I'm not alone in trying to understand how to navigate conflict among my family members, friends, coworkers, and others in the bigger communities of which I'm a part. We're living in an era of polarization when questions and fears like mine come up every day.

I want to try to answer some of those questions and address some of those fears.

To help you understand how to prepare for and successfully navigate conflict, I'd first like to explore some essential *definitions, feelings, and thought processes,* all of which contribute to the way we understand each other and behave when it comes to conflict. Throughout the book, I'll share my own insights and research about the main drivers of conflict, including cultural beliefs that influence how we respond to each other in conflict situations.

Defining *Conflict*, *Contention*, and *Peace*

As I said in the Preface, the simplest definition of conflict is "differences that matter" to one or more parties. In our daily lives, we can easily become involved in a conflict without even knowing if another person *assumes a difference* between us. From making an unpopular political remark online to cutting someone off while driving or simply bumping into someone in the grocery store line, we don't always know what will create conflict for us or other people.

Conflict theorists Kenneth W. Thomas and Ralph H. Kilmann—best known for creating a personal conflict style assessment tool—elaborate on the nuances of conflict by defining it as "a situation in which two or more persons' concerns are or appear to be incompatible, and bad feelings may be involved."[4] In other words, it's natural that people will have incompatible concerns, and it's also natural to misunderstand other people's concerns. This leads to the *appearance* of a conflict, even when none really exists.

Have you ever read through an upsetting news article and gotten all riled up about the state of the world only to learn through Snopes or FactCheck.org that you had been fed misinformation? Getting clear, accurate information is the first step to understanding whether or not a conflict is real or fictional.

Other definitions of conflict focus *on our actions,* or what we do as a result of conflict, as well as the *negative feelings* we experience and express. Think about the tension you felt when that lady cut you off in traffic and you glared back at the "idiot" behind the wheel, speeding around her with your lights flashing. Or that one old guy who always fouls you way too hard while playing pick-up basketball games at the gym. During the heat of the moment, you experience the pushing, shoving, and yelling (actions) and a lot of frustration, anger, and insult (negative feelings) when people—even strangers—act with disrespect toward you. It's always hard to ignore negative actions and feelings directed at you.

In any conflict, you'll face the challenge of sorting out real incompatibilities from what is only *perceived* as incompatible. You'll also have to figure out what to actually do about your conflicts and how to handle all the strong feelings that come with it.

Despite its potential for generating bad feelings, conflict is neither good nor bad. Our experiences of conflict don't have to involve negative feelings or become contentious. We experience natural "differences"—like bumping into another person while playing a sport or voicing an awkward or unpopular opinion in a staff meeting—because we operate with limited information and skills. We don't know what's in other people's minds or how to reach a reasonable solution. Instead of checking in for meaning, too often we puff our chests, shrink back in shame, or try to humiliate another person into displaying our desired behaviors.

Misunderstandings and accidents happen, and they make us feel bad. We drop things, voice dissenting opinions, slip on the ice, fail a math test, and even crash into other cars on the highway. Conflicts like these are a part and parcel of the human world.

But contention is a choice.

When we experience conflict and develop hostile feelings toward another person because they've pushed against us at the local discount store, contention begins. While conflict centers around a difference or friction, contention involves an added layer of negative emotion such as anger, resentment, or hostility.

Remember: Contention and conflict are different terms and experiences.

And *peace* is entirely different from both contention and conflict. Peace involves feelings and experiences of *serenity, calm, and harmony* rather than merely an absence of conflict. As author and journalist Dorothy Thompson said, "Peace is not the absence of conflict, but the presence of creative alternatives for responding to conflict."[5]

Peace is a natural by-product of constructive conflict resolution, which involves building understanding by meeting real needs and wants and preserving the dignity and respect of others. We *create* peace rather than waiting for it to rise out of thin air.

And by the way, everyone around you doesn't have to agree with you to create peace, but collective peace certainly *enhances* your experiences of personal peace. You could feel completely at peace while sitting next to a silent stranger who is in utter turmoil. You'd be affected by the stranger's experience of turmoil, but the stranger could not destroy your own experience of peace without your consent.

Feeling Conflict

Conflict is a natural part of our lives, but it can be overwhelming when we're unprepared for it. Right now, we live in a society steeped in destructive patterns of conflict and contention. Despite our deep desire for peace and understanding, we often fall into traps that stop us from overcoming our differences and building understanding and connection with others.

Conflict can feel like a wide variety of emotions, including *surprise, confusion, anxiety, tension, anger, fear, and shame.* Just thinking about a significant personal conflict can make your blood pressure rise, your chest tighten, and keep you up at night. When you're in intense conflict, your rational brain may even shut down, letting strong, scary emotions take over.

Remember my uncomfortable political conversation with friends? My emotions in that case became increasingly negative so that I needed time and reflection to sort out the issues that had fueled my responses during the conversation. I felt cornered, so I ran away.

In retrospect, I see that I actually felt unsure about some of my beliefs, and I had very little experience talking through issues with people who were on the opposite side. This was uncharted territory for me. I needed more tools than I had in my personal kit that night. I needed to step away to understand how the conflict began and then process my hostile feelings and strong emotions.

While we usually understand something about how our intense feelings arise in a particular conflict, we may be less conscious of our *thought processes* and our own unique, tried-and-true patterns in responding to conflict.

Thinking Conflict

As human beings, we're wired, first and foremost, to meet our own personal needs and create social connections with others. We're also thinking creatures who want to apply reason to problems we face. Because we're each unique, we naturally experience differences, or friction, that threaten the delicate balance between meeting our own needs and being loved by others.

For example, in one moment, I want to work in silence in my office, but fifteen minutes later, I long to have a conversation (social connection) with my husband, friend, or children. There is nothing wrong with us when we experience competing internal thoughts; we just need to recognize that we're wired to seek both *independence and connection*.

Despite the various roles we play and the different relationships we enjoy, all of us—often unconsciously—are constantly trying to balance between meeting our individual needs and making sure we have strong social connections with others. Considering this tension, we should not be surprised that in almost every human relationship (even with ourselves), we experience conflict. Rather than ignoring the tension, we benefit by acknowledging competing thoughts in ourselves and in every other person we meet. This central tension between independence and connection underlies all discussion of conflict and the Five Conflict Approaches to come.

How the Book Is Organized

In Chapter 1 of *Conflict Fluent,* I'll begin by asking you to think about some big picture questions related to conflict in the world and in your own life. I'll include a series of Questions for Reflection that will help you understand your own relationship to conflict in a deeper way.

In each of the five chapters that follow, I'll share some stories and explain one of the five essential approaches to conflict. I'll end each of these chapters with more Questions for Reflection.

You'll probably want to keep your own journal or notebook in which to answer the reflection questions and jot down thoughts, intentions, and goals. I'll repeat the key takeaways in a short summary at the end of each chapter so you can reference the ideas later on your own journey toward conflict fluency.

A concluding chapter will synthesize the learning we've done together and send you off with a few more ideas for practicing conflict fluency on your own.

Let's get started.

QUESTIONS FOR REFLECTION

1. How do I define conflict?

2. When have I experienced conflict without negative feelings?

3. How do I distinguish a conflict from contention, a disagreement, or a dispute?

4. When do I experience peace in my life?

5. How do I describe that peace?

Chapter 1

The Roots and Branches of Conflict

Most conflict stems from the same root cause: perceived or actual incompatible goals. Goal incompatibility means that *two or more people want, or appear to want, the same or different things*. Whether we both want the last piece of pie, or one partner wants to downsize while the other wants to stay put, we are experiencing goal incompatibility.

According to Dr. Otomar J. Bartos and Dr. Paul Wehr, three fundamental situations feed into our incompatible goals:

- *Contested Resources:* When we perceive and want what appear to be limited resources such as money, power, personal time, or prestige.

- *Incompatible Roles*: When we play roles with natural tension or imbalanced power.

- *Incompatible Values*: When we have different views of the world, which result in our wanting different outcomes.[6]

In this chapter, we'll review each of these deep roots of goal incompatibility so you can better understand your experiences of conflict. We'll look at the impact of mental and physical health on conflict, and then we'll look at the social and cultural context in which our conflicts play out.

Contested Resources: Trying to Get Your Share of a Small Pie

We live in a society in which we all compete for resources, such as money, quality time, power, prestige, and even affection. We swerve past strangers to get the best parking spot, compete with colleagues to get the promotion, and even fight with family members for the last Diet Coke left in the fridge. Whether we like it or not, we often feel compelled to compete with others to make sure we don't miss out on something valuable.

Having survived 2020, I will probably always buy toilet paper when I go into a grocery store, just to be sure that I don't get left empty-handed. In conflicts involving contested resources, we tend to believe there is only so much pie (or toilet paper) to divide, so we try to get as much for ourselves as we can. Our experiences teach us that there are real winners and losers in society, and we want to be winners.

But sometimes we act as if something is scarce, even though it's not. You may chase power and authority at work, believing that if someone else has it, you'll go without. Sometimes there are only two movie tickets left for opening night or only 500 spots available in the Harvard Business School class, but more often than not, we're deceived by *perceptions* of scarcity. In other words, the pie is not as small as we think it is.

When everyone in the United States started hoarding bottled water in March 2020, my state's governor had to remind us that we could still get unlimited clean water from our taps. There was plenty of water to go around, but mass hysteria led to a perception of scarcity. Naturally, shoppers experienced serious frustration when they couldn't find bottled water on the shelves of any nearby grocery stores, but water was not *really* scarce, and their basic human survival wasn't threatened.

Beyond asking whether a conflict over contested tangible resources is real or just perceived, you should also pay attention to how you compete over intangible things such as love, attention, and recognition. Often, we also compete for opportunities, like a promotion at work. Have you ever stayed in a job you hate just waiting for a promotion, even though you know that nobody's been promoted from your department in years? We all benefit by accepting that certain resources truly *are* finite, so we don't spend our time waiting for something that will never materialize.

A healthy reality check based on facts can help you make better decisions about situations with truly scarce resources or limited opportunities. Consider the questions below to generate your own thoughts about the tangible and intangible resources, opportunities, and time you compete for in your life.

Questions for Reflection

1. What are the contested resources in my home life?

2. What are the contested resources in my work life?

3. How do the members of my family compete for limited resources such as time, money, privileges, and parental attention?

4. Is there anything I'd like to change now about how I deal with or distribute contested resources in a certain area of my life?

5. Are there any areas of contested resources in my life that are mostly perceived rather than real?

Incompatible Roles: Dealing with the Power Imbalances in Your Life

The roles we play often naturally pit us against each other. For example, in a basketball game, my role as a player sets me against a player from the other team and perhaps also against a referee from another league. I want to score against the defender and don't want the ref to call a foul on me. In a competitive sport, we understand that players are battling against each other under the watchful eye of a referee who is trying to maintain a neutral stance and ensure a fair game. We understand that Team A wants to beat Team B and vice versa, and we usually know if one team is favored to win by virtue of its stronger players or better record. We aren't troubled by those competitive roles and imbalances of power because that's what we expect in a sport or game.

But at home, work, or even in politics, we're often troubled by conflicting or incompatible roles. Parents and teenagers are in conflict over curfews, chores, and driving privileges. These days, parents often behave more like friends to their teenagers, but what if your teenager grows increasingly depressed, won't leave his room, and refuses to talk with you?

As a parent, you're concerned about your child's mental health, but your teenage son just wants physical and emotional freedom without being told what to do. Certainly, compromise is possible in some situations, but there's a power imbalance that complicates things on both sides.

My friend Megan struggled with a frightening situation that involved her son's desire to commit suicide. She had to carefully walk the line between concerned parent and trusted confidante while seeking the professional support her son needed. In tenuous situations like Megan's, parents try to respect their children's autonomy while safeguarding their children's lives. My heart goes out to parents who find themselves in these perilous situations where they must flexibly shift roles and modify their parental authority to ensure their child's well-being.

When certain roles become our primary sources of identity, we tend to experience more conflict than usual. As a general rule, we resist making compromises regarding our primary sources of identity, and in families, that often means our identity as a parent or a child. We'll address these roles more in later chapters.

Although it's often less obvious, we also struggle when our family's social roles lack adequate definition. Our lack of defined roles leads to confusion and unexpressed expectations. At work, in your home, or out in your community, you need to communicate explicitly about all your roles to create understanding. When both parents work, who makes the dinner each night? Or, who's really the top dog among the middle managers reporting to a single VP? Does everyone have equal footing, or has one manager earned a special place of trust and influence above the others? When there is a lack of definition and unclear expectations, we tend to struggle.

In regular daily life, we experience conflict fueled by incompatible roles, especially when natural or traditional power imbalances rock our social roles. Consider the potential tension for a friend of mine, Brooke, who asked her boss, Wayne, for a raise. Brooke had no authority to set her own wages, and as a woman in a world of male executives, she worried about being perceived as too aggressive if she made many demands. Brooke's roles "under" her boss and as a woman in a pool of male leaders invited possible tension related to role incompatibility.

To begin working through the tension, Brooke approached Wayne cautiously, knowing he could fire her if she was out of line. She prepared by researching out what numbers might be appropriate. When she finally asked Wayne for a raise, he said he was restricted because his department director controlled the budget, but that he was willing to advocate for her because he didn't want to lose such a good employee.

Brooke and Wayne experienced different role restrictions and behaved within power structures that heavily influenced how they could resolve the issue. In the end, despite any apparent limitations created by their differing roles, they managed to cooperate with each other rather than remain at an impasse. Brooke created materials to validate her work contributions, which Wayne could then present to his boss to demonstrate why Brooke deserved a raise. They both had to wait for a new budgeting cycle to open up before they could take action on their plan, but waiting proved useful. By asserting their needs *and* working within the hierarchy, both Wayne and Brooke achieved their goals.

If you experience power in your primary social roles, you can assume that if you regularly assert your authority at home, work, and in the community, people will learn to strategically respond to your displays of power—and possibly try to go around you. Children, employees, congregants, and even strangers may learn to *imitate*, or mirror, your displays of power and approaches to conflict and use them against you. Don't be too surprised when those "under" you start imitating how you use power when they gain power themselves. Subordinates often mirror the conflict approaches their authority figures use.

To prevent or resolve unnecessary conflict generated by role incompatibility, consider ways you can balance power and soften natural sources of role tension in your relationships—even with strangers. Rather than seeing ourselves as opponents in an imbalanced power situation, we can learn to work *side-by-side* with others as *joint* problem solvers.

When you're in a position of authority, instead of trying to solve everyone else's problems, try supporting them as they try to solve their own.

Wayne worked with Brooke to secure the raise she needed, but requested her help to convince his boss that she was deserving. He relied on her research to present the request to his boss in the most appropriate way within the power hierarchy. In the end, goal incompatibility played a role in Brooke's and Wayne's interactions with each other, but did not ultimately prevent them from working together as a sign of their mutual respect and confidence.

Questions for Reflection

1. What are the main roles I play in my daily life?

2. In which roles do I experience role incompatibility or differences in power?

3. How do I handle role incompatibility and/or power differences in my relationships?

4. In my family, work, or community life, which relationships include equal power differentials?

5. How am I trying to balance power differentials in my work, home, and community life?

Incompatible Values: Wanting Different Things Leads to Conflict

Sometimes we experience conflict with each other because as unique individuals with diverse perspectives, attitudes, and behaviors, we have incompatible values and beliefs. For example, you love off-roading in your ATV over Bureau of Land Management deserts, while I support an environmental group seeking to safeguard those lands.

We need to be careful not to confuse ordinary differences of taste, style, and resolution methods with more serious disputes about incompatible values. Too often, we experience conflict because of our *perceptions* of incompatible values when real solutions involving compromise and greater understanding are possible.

In mediation, I see people unwilling to seek resolution because they claim that their values are just too different from the other person's. This type of thinking is usually overly simplistic and leads to a lack of communication and stalemates. Sometimes, you just need to suspend your perception of value conflicts and hear the other person out. Usually, the person you're in conflict with has some rational basis for their thoughts, opinions, and actions.

For example, I may enjoy relaxing to the sounds of soft acoustic guitar music after work, while my roommate likes to unwind with heavy metal turned up to an ear-splitting level. We both value music and use it to transition from work to home. If we communicate about our shared values, it's more likely we can come up with ways we can meet both of our needs, maybe with headphones, staggered listening schedules, or some other solution.

In the contentious world of politics, both political parties want to provide physical safety, strong educational opportunities for children, robust economic growth and prosperity. However, many of us jump to the conclusion that different values and beliefs make it impossible for us to get along with members of a different political party. As a result, we avoid resolving conflicts at all, when there is actually enough overlap between parties to reach resolution on many fronts. The key is to approach others' values and beliefs with an eye toward identifying overlapping or *common* areas of belief rather than focusing solely on differences.

If we lay aside our preconceptions, we often discover we're dead wrong in our initial assessments of each other because we didn't take the time to listen and learn.

If we can even *imagine* the possibility of common ground, we're much more likely to work through any real or perceived value or belief differences we may encounter. We may not *always* find common ground because our values still differ, but we shouldn't prematurely assume our conflict involves opposing values rather than lots of perceived differences. The fact is, our interests often overlap even if our proposed solutions do not.

Skillful communication can help us uncover hidden common ground that we can't see in the heat of an argument.

Conflict resolution specialists Dr. Michael Spangle and Dr. Myra Isenhart suggest that even when we don't have actual conflicts related to contested resources, incompatible roles, or incompatible values, we might disagree on *how* to resolve our differences.[7] Consider these four areas of disagreement when you're working out a dispute, and figure out if you can reach an agreement on the "how:"

- *Information:* Do you disagree about what information is correct or what standards should be used for judging who's right or wrong?

- *Procedures:* Do you and the other person or group agree on which method to use to solve a problem, make decisions, or resolve a conflict?

- *Relationships:* Do you trust, respect, and believe in the honesty of the other person or people?

- *Communication:* Do you phrase your conflict, problem, or question to avoid creating more contention and defensiveness in others?[8]

Ideally, we would all outline what information counts, build trust with those with whom we are in conflict, and agree on what procedure(s) and kinds of communication will be used *before* a conflict occurs.

For example, when considering the needs and differences between the ATV-er and the environmentalist, both parties are more likely to reach compromise solutions when they focus on using effective conflict resolution procedures, establishing relationships of trust, communicating clearly, and sharing their sources of information. Rather than concentrating merely on our easy-to-spot value differences, when we dig deeper, we may uncover a shared love for nature, adventure, and autonomy.

When we take these areas into account, we waste less time and are more likely to work through our differences.

Questions for Reflection

1. With whom do I have regular conflicts over incompatible values?

2. Is there an overlap of values despite my perception of incompatibility? If so, where is the overlap?

3. How do information, procedures, relationships, and communication preferences play into conflicts I've experienced or am experiencing now?

How Mental and Physical Health Affect Conflict Patterns

I won't address health issues in detail in this book, but I'd urge you to consider how addiction, mental or physical pain, illness, hunger, thirst, fatigue, and stress factor into your conflict resolution approaches.

When we have unmet needs or are abusing ourselves or others, we often live in a state of conflict, regardless of other people's behavior. In effect, we're in conflict with ourselves all the time. Our personal adversities dramatically affect our ability to deal with conflict constructively and lead to greater conflict and contention than we'd otherwise experience. We must address these personal problems before or during the time we're trying to change our interactions with others in conflict situations.

After a year of successfully avoiding the coronavirus, my husband and I both became sick in April 2021. We relied mostly on our oldest child to serve us three meals a day and keep the family going while we self-isolated in another part of the house. While in an achy stupor, I began ruminating about some important changes I wanted to make in our family interactions to build more love and connection. But during nearly 10 days in isolation, I realized that I shouldn't make any big decisions at that moment. I needed to focus on making a full recovery and deal with my family concerns when I had a less cloudy outlook and more energy to give to my treasured relationships.

Once healed, I realized that some of my concerns were more imagined than real. If I had tried to make big changes to my family dynamic while sick, I might have caused turmoil instead of creating more connection.

If you, a loved one, or someone you interact with regularly experiences significant personal challenges, please actively address these issues as you're considering conflict resolution. Seek individual support from trained professionals who can help you resolve the inner struggles that deeply affect your social interactions at home, work, and school. Addressing these issues head on can make a great positive difference.

Please see the Appendix under "Mental Health Resources" if you, or someone you know, is struggling with depression, anxiety, addiction, or another mental health challenge.

Questions for Reflection

---

1. Do I have any outstanding personal issues that are fueling conflicts in my life? If so, describe those issues.

2. What are some paths by which I can start to resolve those issues?

3. Do I—or some of the people I interact with most often—have habits, challenges, or illnesses that affect the conflict climate in my home, at work, or in the community?

4. How am I addressing negative personal habits or situations to improve the situation?

Social and Cultural Influences on Conflict

In every country, the social and cultural climate influences how people think about and behave in conflict. In the United States and around the world in the 21st century, we're inundated with news images of civil strife, war, terrorism, and abuse, as well as violent fictional entertainment. With our eyes wide open to our social and cultural context, we can better understand the influences at work on our attitudes and perceptions about conflict from childhood through adulthood. Some of the most important aspects of our current social and cultural context are:

- *The media primes us for accepting violence:* In our culture, we consume mass quantities of violence in our entertainment, whether we're watching movies and TV, reading books, listening to music, or playing video games. Although we complain about how depressing and scary the news is, we often choose violent entertainment for personal pleasure. We cannot help but be influenced by what we take in visually and aurally in all forms of media.

- *Underreacting, overreacting, and delaying:* Beyond consuming violent media as news or entertainment, the social context we live in often leads us to reject dealing with daily conflict in a tempered way. Instead of resolving a conflict with a loved one, many of us underreact or delay, giving in to addictions, gossip, the silent treatment, or even moving thousands of miles away to extinguish the possibility of contact. But we can figuratively "hold our breath" for only so long, especially regarding issues that we care deeply about.

We may escalate small conflicts into volatile situations that require professional intervention because we *wait* until we're overwhelmed before seeking help. An ounce of attention or prevention goes a long way toward avoiding unnecessary explosions. I always tell clients: Don't procrastinate!

On the flip side, some of us *overreact* and escalate minor conflicts into major disagreements with higher stakes.

One afternoon, I met in my office with an anxious young man who was terrified when he received an official police letter ordering him to avoid any contact with his ex-girlfriend. Believing the police letter had the force of a restraining order, he was worried about walking around his college campus because he risked running into his ex. He wondered if he now had a police record.

After careful conversation with him and the policeman who crafted the letter, I learned that this young man had never threatened any violence toward his ex-girlfriend. Most likely, she had simply wanted to break-up with him but didn't know how to do it on her own. By contacting the police rather than going through the awkwardness of breaking up with her boyfriend face-to-face, she provoked serious anxiety in an otherwise harmless person. This may not always be the case, but in this situation, the formal letter was an overreaction.

- *Weaknesses in social institutions:* If we look closely, we can see that many of our social institutions, including schools, churches, recreation centers, and workplaces, are just not set up for everyday conflict resolution. Instead of simplifying our approaches and addressing conflict at the individual or neighborhood level, we too often bring them to the courts and legal system—the most costly and time-consuming solutions.

How would our lives be improved if we assumed (and prepared for) the ongoing need for conflict resolution in our homes, schools, and workplaces rather than turning to a higher, more distant authority?

Questions for Reflection

1. How am I consuming violence as entertainment in my life?

2. When do I tend to either underreact or overreact to conflict?

3. When am I more likely to delay responding to conflict?

4. What plans are in place at work to deal with conflict? At home? In my community?

Constructive, Close-to-Home Solutions

In the next chapters, we'll explore the Five Conflict Approaches that I believe can lead us toward conflict fluency. We'll learn how to use these approaches in ways that are *constructive rather than destructive,* and we'll study them in examples that take place *close to home,* not in some distant setting where we're surrounded by strangers.

By teaching you the basics of conflict fluency, I want to discourage the most destructive approaches to conflict, which are personal attacks and expressions of hostile emotions like contempt and domination of one person over another. These destructive approaches focus on winners and losers, break down group cohesion, and criticize others' ideas. They also tend to promote the domination of a larger group, leading toward more conformity and less creativity.[9]

On the other hand, the Five Conflict Approaches and conflict fluency are *constructive.* They focus on defining clear interests, ideas, and tasks. Positive approaches to conflict resolution generate discovery, creativity, and better decision-making.

I hope these approaches will help empower you and strengthen our collective commitment to families, schools, churches, community organizations, and workplaces that do the same.

AN OVERVIEW OF THE ROOTS
AND BRANCHES OF CONFLICT:

THINGS TO REMEMBER

Conflict is a situation in which two or more people's concerns *appear* to be incompatible, which may create bad feelings between them.

What influences our perceived or real incompatible goals:

- *Contested Resources:* We desire money, power, personal time, prestige, or other resources that appear to be limited.
- *Incompatible Roles:* We play roles in which we experience power imbalances.
- *Incompatible Values:* We have different views of the world, leading us to want different things.

Disagreements over resolving conflicts involve:

- *Information:* We disagree about what information is correct or what standards should be used to make and judge decisions.
- *Procedures:* We disagree on the best method to solve a problem, make a decision, or resolve a conflict.
- *Relationships:* We lack trust, respect, or a belief in the honesty of the person or people on the other side of a conflict.

- *Communication*: We phrase our conflict, problem, or question in a way that leads to misunderstandings.

Patterns and assumptions around conflict include:

- *Media that Prime Us for Violence*: In our culture, we accept violence as entertainment and often lack the skills to resolve our daily conflicts without violence.
- *Urgent Instead of Preventive Care*: We often wait until a small problem has grown large before trying to resolve it.
- *Social Institutions that Don't Know How to Deal with Conflict*: Most of our institutions don't have good conflict resolution practices outside the legal system.

Differences between constructive and destructive conflict:

Constructive Conflict:
- Focuses on interests, ideas, and tasks.
- Generates discovery, creativity, better decision-making, and empowerment of others, while strengthening the commitment to an organization.

Destructive Conflict:
- Focuses on people and emotions to assert domination.
- Generates winners and losers, destroys group cohesion, criticizes ideas, promotes the domination of a group, and leads to group conformity.

Chapter 2

Conflict Approach #1: Avoiding

As a lowly fourth grader taking violin lessons for the first time, I felt a little anxious just walking into Ms. Lee's fifth/sixth-grade classroom for orchestra. Rumor had it this teacher would rage and punish kids with 1,000-word papers—and even cancel recess entirely! I didn't know Ms. Lee, but I didn't want to test her and find out if the rumors were true.

At the end of orchestra time on that first morning, I couldn't put down my music stand. I looked around to ask for help from my orchestra-mates, but everyone had already packed up and left. After struggling, I managed to disassemble the top part of the metal stand, but I had to leave the bottom part open by the supply room door. I just couldn't get it to close right. I'd set it down carefully and neatly, so I assumed I was safe from Ms. Lee's ire and returned to Mrs. Schmidt's fourth-grade classroom in the nearby portable.

About 15 minutes after returning to class, I shuddered as two student messengers from Ms. Lee's class entered our classroom and announced, "All students who had orchestra in Ms. Lee's classroom need to come with us right now."

Not knowing the reason for the summons but dreading the worst, I nervously marched with my classmates to her room where all the older fifth and sixth graders' eyes locked on us. I saw a few of the older boys smirking. Arriving in a group was comforting for about a minute, until I noticed the bottom half of my music stand perched at the front of the classroom by Ms. Lee's desk.

She had put my crime on display for everyone to see.

With the entire classroom watching, Ms. Lee questioned all the summoned students like a judge in a court of law. "Who was so rude to have left this stand open? Come forward and admit what you've done," she bellowed.

No one said anything. I was paralyzed. Why would I, or anyone else, want to speak up and risk public humiliation and punishment?

I was so afraid that I can only recall moving in a frightened clump with a few others toward the music stand per Ms. Lee's orders. As a group, we struggled for a couple minutes, trying to close the stand beneath her towering presence. (She was actually quite short for an adult woman). Finally, we succeeded in taking the stand down. With a few threats, including, "Don't let me ever see you do this again!" Ms. Lee dismissed us to our classrooms.

I can still recall the terrible feelings of anxiety Ms. Lee's inquisition instilled in me. I wanted to be honest about my mistakes, but the idea of admitting my guilt to Ms. Lee was just too costly. She'd shown her true colors by shaming all the orchestra members as a group, so I assumed that she would probably make life even more difficult for me if I decided to come clean. I never did.

As a young girl moving into adolescence, experiences like these taught me to avoid similar situations by scrupulously following the rules, avoiding contentious people, and sometimes not admitting my mistakes. Most of the time, I could skirt individuals known for bad tempers and try to smooth people's feelings with consoling words, kind actions, and well-mannered behavior. As a teenager, I had occasional run-ins with ornery people, but generally, I associated with those who treated me well—the fewer Ms. Lee types, I thought, the better.

While this simple avoidance strategy worked fairly well in protecting me from contentious people and situations for a long time, my relationships and challenges became more complex as a young adult. In college and then the workplace, I couldn't so easily avoid difficult people. They came into my life in the form of roommates, coworkers, and bosses. As my need for intimacy and friendship changed, so did the variety of responses I had to develop and manage.

Maybe you never had a traumatic encounter with a teacher like Ms. Lee, but have you ever hidden in a grocery store when you saw someone you knew but didn't want to talk to? What about all the phone calls that you let ring to voicemail, the emails you somehow missed despite their urgent nature, and the texts you left unanswered because you didn't know how to respond? Of course, we're all subject to forgetfulness and get overwhelmed by life, but if we're honest, we also *choose* to avoid confronting touchy, difficult, sad, or otherwise "unfun" situations.

If we're lucky, some of our conflicts go away by avoiding them, but research suggests that most family conflicts remain unresolved if avoided, including conflicts between parents and children, spouses, and siblings. When we avoid resolving important issues, our conflicts may only get more intense and come back with greater frequency, which definitely does not lead to more connection and peace in our lives. Remember that any overused conflict approach from our five choices can lead to relationship imbalances and result in a lack of intimacy and connection, even if our intentions are loving and kind.

As a seasoned but mostly recovered chronic avoider, I'm familiar with the landscape of the Avoiding Approach. You may be quite comfortable on this path, which leads us to take flight quickly or calmly retreat when we encounter any conflicts. For example, when someone brings up home budgeting, getting a flu shot, or the fact that they didn't like my performance at work, my avoidance instinct might kick in.

Despite having this initial desire to run from conflict, with practice, I've learned to manage the urge and thoughtfully consider whether I should retreat or withhold responding. I've learned to restrain myself from giving in to a knee-jerk avoidance reaction as my primary conflict resolution strategy, because I don't want to fall back into old patterns that haven't always served me well.

But I still believe the Avoidance Approach has a rightful place in our conflict resolution tool kit. We never want to go too far in our course corrections that we dismiss a legitimate tool that works well in some situations.

Let's explore the Avoiding Approach in more detail now.

What Is the Avoiding Approach?

When we avoid conflict, we don't directly address the subject or the people involved. Instead, we change the topic of conversation when it becomes uncomfortable, stop responding to or discussing issues, become noncommittal, and even end any type of contact. When we're avoiding, we don't openly seek to satisfy our own needs or the other person's needs.

Of course, we may have a specific personal or altruistic goal that motivates us to use an Avoiding Approach, but it can often be simply the path of least resistance.

When and why do people usually use the Avoiding Approach?

When I was a junior in high school, I always looked forward to my English class with Mr. Thompson. He had a quick wit and engaging teaching style that usually led to interesting debates among my classmates about all kinds of topics.

On one particular morning, as I sat down, ready to participate in our literature discussion, Mr. Thompson began the class, "As we all know, religious people are just looking for a crutch to explain their suffering."

I was shocked. I don't think I heard much of what followed for a minute or two. As a religious teenager in a largely secular community in Northern California, I had never encountered such a public affront to my belief in a classroom setting before. I wasn't prepared to say anything in response to contradict my teacher, so I stayed silent. After Mr. Thompson paused, one of the more popular boys in my class, Jack, chose to speak up.

"Hey, Mr. Thompson, I think there might be some religious people here who would disagree with what you just said."

I admired Jack's courage in defending a person like me, especially because I knew he didn't share my religious beliefs. But I still didn't say anything. I just assumed that hardly anyone felt the way I did about God and faith, so why bother making myself potentially unpopular and sticking out in the crowd?

The topic of discussion in Mr. Thompson's class eventually shifted and we never really returned to it, so my willingness to engage in conflict wasn't tested again in that context. But avoiding important topics in our lives often comes with a price. For 30 years since that day, I've regretted my silence. While I've forgiven myself for not speaking up, I wish that I had possessed the confidence to voice my deep religious belief in an academic setting at that time. I didn't need to speak up to convince anyone of the validity of my beliefs, but I should have stood up for *myself* instead of avoiding being seen for who I really am: a religious minority. Instead, I learned to completely separate my religious and academic truths until much later in my life.

My high school English class experience taught me the necessity of owning and representing my beliefs rather than avoiding confrontation with people who might disagree with me. While remaining silent might be appropriate in other situations, in this classroom setting, I knew from my own gut reaction that I had diminished my self-respect at a pivotal juncture in the evolution of my maturity. I needed to speak up for myself more than for others to hear what I had to say.

But avoiding conflict isn't always the wrong choice. In the early 1990s, I studied for five months in Jerusalem with Brigham Young University's Center for Near Eastern Studies. In order to build the BYU Center on Mt. Scopus in Jerusalem, The Church of Jesus Christ of Latter-day Saints (the Mormons) had made an official agreement with the government of Israel not to engage in any type of mission or evangelizing work in the Holy Land. Each student who attended the Jerusalem study abroad program was required to sign an individual written agreement not to proselytize. In practice, this meant that our large group of 180 American Mormons roaming around Jerusalem, throughout Israel and Palestine and into Egypt, kept our answers simple when people questioned us about who we were. We all kept our individual commitments and avoided talking about our religion. In that case, the Avoiding Approach was the right one.

Many of us naturally gravitate toward the Avoiding Approach in both close interpersonal conflicts and larger group situations because we understand that avoiding confrontation is *expected* of us. We may be involved in power relationships and patterns that pressure us to avoid conflict, especially conflict with people in authority.

Some of us avoid conflict when we think we have little power to influence how issues will be resolved. If my boss decides that my project is no good, I might not give her a piece of my mind and stand up for myself because she could fire me or put me on a project I like much less. Likewise, if I'm appearing in a traffic court before a black-robed judge behind a five-foot-high desk, I'm more likely to avoid confrontation, acknowledge my wrongs, and plead for mercy. In large-scale community situations, we might consider whether low voter turnout and large numbers of high school dropouts reflect avoidance patterns at some level and ask ourselves why.

In other words, when we hold less power than the individuals or groups we are interacting with, we are more likely to avoid confrontation in conflict. We think, "Why waste the time and energy in a no-win situation?"

On the flip side, I am much more likely to confront someone, rather than avoid them, if I have *social power* of some kind. Social power can include being an upperclassman in high school, the respected grandfather in a family, or a manager at work. Power simply means that I have the ability to influence outcomes.

Imagine all of the parents across the world telling their kids how to improve and to help more with chores without thinking for a moment about avoiding confrontation. In the workplace, consider all of the supervisors and bosses who give job reviews, carry out interviews, divvy up work tasks, and even decide how conflict should be resolved between employees. In government, power influences politicians jockeying for position and their attempts to sway public opinion to resolve or heighten conflicts.

If I have seniority and social status on my side, I may feel it is my right to make course corrections for groups I oversee without even acknowledging the troubles or conflicts I'm creating for those with less power. In cases where authority, seniority, and status converge, I can make big demands on those around me.

I might say something like, "Kids, get your chores done by noon. I don't care what you have going on. Just do it."

Research suggests that this isn't unusual. When we have a lot of power, we spend little time thinking about those with less power. We simply don't see their obstacles as clearly as our own. On one hand, when we feel and experience power, we are often blind to the potential harm we're causing for others. On the other hand, those with less power will avoid confronting powerful people about real problems because they think it will be fruitless. You can see how this can lead to all kinds of societal unrest and dissatisfaction with the people in power.

Have you ever thought about how you've been taught to avoid discussing taboo topics like politics, religion, international policy, and marital relationships, because they are complicated or sensitive? Sometimes certain topics just create more social friction than we believe we can comfortably handle.

While there's wisdom in staying a safe distance from a hot flame, we will soon explore how avoiding *all* hard topics can lead to real human heartache and problems across society. We can't avoid every taboo subject and still have the connections with people that we need and want.

Power dynamics definitely influence whether we avoid or confront conflict, but a lot of us avoid conflict in our daily lives in order to be kind and compassionate. If I care about you and notice that you're not ready to talk about a deep conflict issue, I might avoid bringing it up until I know you're ready and willing to talk. I may see the pain in your eyes and understand that you need time and space to focus your energies elsewhere. With patience on my side, I expect that sometime soon we will work on our conflict.

When I'm starting a new relationship with someone, I may avoid asking overly sensitive questions because I understand that we need a foundation of trust and understanding before we tackle harder, more personal topics. For example, I might avoid a discussion about why you got divorced until we've reached our third or fourth date, because I want you to feel comfortable and want to confirm to you that I don't see you as flawed or broken.

In many situations like the example above, the Avoiding Approach demonstrates compassion and patience rather than weakness or naivete.

In contrast to avoiding conflict out of love and respect for someone else's sensitivities and timetable, sometimes we avoid conflicts because we don't care that much about the relationship. I may be completely apathetic about your concerns, so I don't answer when you come knocking at my door about a political cause. I may skirt across the conference room to engage in conversation with someone else during a staff meeting, or I may simply look away when you try to catch my eye at the movie theater. In all of these cases, I don't want to put any effort into the relationship at that moment, including any conflicts we might have, so I avoid you.

If one side of the spectrum is apathy, the other side is anger. I might completely avoid dealing with our conflicts if I don't trust my ability to control my temper, or if I believe you will lose control of yours. Either way, I fear things spiraling out of control, so I avoid confrontations at all costs.

Most of us try to avoid danger, including people who have or could hurt us, physically, mentally, emotionally, or otherwise. When we avoid people we love because we fear the rejection and potential fallout if our expectations are dashed, we're reacting to perceived emotional dangers—

even if the people we're dealing with are not necessarily fearsome.

Whether out of love or fear, consider how your perception of power plays into your interpersonal patterns of avoidance. A dance of power and influence is happening around all conflicts, even when both parties long to resolve them. Rather than avoiding conflict because we fear the hard conversations, or we believe we'll be wasting our time, we need to use the Avoiding Approach only in appropriate circumstances, which I'll talk about below.

Let's now look at some of the clearest benefits and drawbacks of using the Avoiding Approach.

What are the benefits of using the Avoiding Approach?

On a cold winter day, Dave sat cozily with his soon-to-be-ex-girlfriend, Eve, in his arms. He wondered if he could delay the dreaded breakup conversation and stay with Eve on that soft white couch for a while longer. But he knew that delaying would just cause her more pain, so he smiled gently and asked,

"What are we doing here when we know we're breaking up soon?"

She laughed and told him not to worry so much.

Dave didn't want to let the moment pass, but he tried to keep the conversation light. He really cared about Eve, and told her he had loved their time together, but something just wasn't right about the relationship. He knew she wanted something serious, but he couldn't commit while they were both still in college.

Finally, he pulled away from her embrace and insisted, "So, what's next?"

Eve's smile disappeared. Although he hadn't said it in so many words, he could tell she knew the relationship was over. They talked for a while longer, until she finally whispered, "Okay. I understand."

Neither said much else before she gently closed the door when he left. Dave wasn't sure how things would go in the coming week when they were sure to bump into each other on campus and among mutual friends.

Eve was just as worried about running into Dave as he was about running into her. Despite her initial show of confidence that everything would be fine, she wasn't sure how to feel or act as an ex-girlfriend. To test the waters, a few days after their official breakup, she went to a casual gathering with mutual friends, knowing Dave would be there. The moment she walked into the house and looked down the hallway, Eve spotted Dave laughing and talking with Greta, a friend who had been public about wanting to date Dave for months.

In that instant, Eve knew that she couldn't bear to be around Dave when they weren't a couple any longer. She couldn't handle watching him fall in love with someone else when her emotions were so raw. Their group of mutual friends was far too small to allow either of them to blend into the crowd.

Instead of confronting the conflict head on, Eve chose to walk out of the party and head home without joining her friends. For her emotional survival, she decided to avoid small gatherings when Dave would be present from that moment on. She hated feeling too weak to handle seeing him, but she had to keep herself together. Over the next few weeks, Eve realized that it was okay that she needed time and space to heal before she could see Dave in a new way. Avoiding him and their conflict gave her a chance to regain strength and re-create her identity without him.

Like Eve and Dave, most of us don't just quickly switch gears when treasured relationships come to an end. With the time, reflection, and perspective that the Avoiding Approach can provide, we can learn new patterns and build up other relationships that have atrophied while we focused exclusively on one dating relationship. Avoiding can also benefit us in other ways, including:

- We escape physical, emotional, or other types of danger by avoiding those who might try to harm or hurt us, whether intentionally or not.

- We don't waste time in relationships and related conflicts that we do not care enough about to invest in heavily.

- We don't expend energy or stress on complex issues that we have little control over.

- We help others feel comfortable and maintain their dignity in our presence despite awkward or tense social situations.

- We may create better and wiser resolutions if we take the time to reflect and cool down before responding.

Avoiding conflict in the right situations shows strength and patience rather than personal weakness.

It makes sense to avoid spending energy on issues that don't matter much to us. But, when we avoid communication entirely, or even "ghost" someone, we usually create a variety of new problems, especially when family and close friends aren't able to achieve closure or connection with us.

In the case of Eve and Dave, they actually had the break-up conversation, which helped them to process and heal. In especially mature break-ups, you might even discuss how you're going to react when you see each other in public as a gesture of goodwill. Telling someone that you're going to avoid them sounds strange, but it can be a merciful gesture, because silence is often devastating.

What are the drawbacks of using the Avoiding Approach?

After my fifth child Lucie was born, I seriously struggled with intense feelings of self-doubt and anxiety. While I had felt some blues for four to six weeks after having each of my babies, the emotional battle after Lucie lasted much longer. No amount of positive self-talk, prayers, scripture study, or even talking with trusted friends helped me overcome the wave of depression that settled over me. I could function somewhat normally while parenting my five young children, but I felt awful and unstable. Stubbornly, I refused to seek out medical attention because I had always been able to come out on top in the past.

Six months after Lucie's birth, I found myself sitting in the office of my OB/GYN, Dr. Hansen, for a routine medical check-up. After taking a few notes about my general health, she simply asked me, "And, Emily, how are you doing?"

Within seconds, I teared up and honestly shared how discouraged I felt on a daily basis. After listening for a few minutes, Dr. Hansen looked me in the eyes and said, "Emily, this is not normal. You don't have to keep suffering like this."

I honestly wanted to solve my problems on my own, but as soon as she said those words, I knew that I couldn't do it alone this time. Avoiding my inner conflict and not getting help was hurting me; I had been avoiding admitting to myself and others that I needed help desperately. When Dr. Hansen provided possible solutions to ease me out of my mental pain, I grasped hold of her offer just in time. She offered just what I needed—a listening ear and some medication.

As I left her office with a prescription in hand for an anti-depressant, I had mixed feelings: some shame for having to admit that I couldn't do everything myself, but also hope that I could find relief.

Years later, I look back on that conversation with my doctor with fondness and gratitude. Her simple question cut through my avoidance pattern and helped me receive the relief that I needed. While I had tried to overcome the seriousness of my situation with all kinds of determined efforts to pull myself out, she offered a solution that completely changed my life. Thanks to opening up to Dr. Hansen, I still enjoy a steady relaxed heartbeat and greater mental clarity when life's troubles beat upon me. Thank heavens I shared my difficulties in that moment when my five young children were depending upon me for constant care and attention.

Have you ever tried to do everything all by yourself to avoid an inner conflict? Have you avoided confronting the reality that you're stuck or unable to get past what's bothering you?

I'm guessing you've already experienced some of the drawbacks of using the Avoiding Approach in the wrong situations. If we avoid too often in our close interpersonal relationships, we suffer because connection comes through sharing our vulnerabilities and working through difficulties to mutual satisfaction. Specifically, we may experience these drawbacks:

- We can miss important windows of opportunity to resolve issues when others are aware of what's going on and invested in finding a solution.

- We may experience the world in a superficial way that prohibits a sense of deep feeling and belonging.

- Important conflict issues may linger, often returning with greater frequency and intensity.

Rather than resolving conflicts, many of us sadly experience inner turmoil and stress because those conflicts remain buried while we're avoiding them. When we bring our most important conflict issues into the light, we put ourselves in a position to move forward and beyond that which has constrained us in the past. We find that we don't need to keep running from the dark clouds within and between us; we have the power to *dispel the darkness* with actual resolutions.

What happens when we overuse the Avoiding Approach?

In Japanese culture, avoiding and accommodating are highly integrated into everyday social interactions. To preserve harmony at home, work, and throughout society, people in junior positions are expected to show deference to their elders and others in authority by avoiding direct confrontation.

My friend Grace personally learned how frustrating overusing avoidance patterns can be when she was training a new native Japanese missionary named Sister Yamada.

About ten years ago, Grace and Sister Yamada worked together 24/7 as full-time missionaries for the Mormon Church in Japan. Grace held the leadership role in the pair, so Sister Yamada avoided any confrontation or disagreement with her. Grace could tell from Sister Yamada's nonverbal behavior—looking away or occasionally sighing—that she disagreed with Grace's leadership decisions, but would not openly confront her. Grace found this Avoiding Approach aggravating because she didn't have anyone to counsel with about hard situations. Grace believed she had inherited a "yes-man" who might silently resent her decisions but would never speak out.

To make matters more complex, Grace was baffled why the mission leadership had assigned a native Japanese speaker to learn from an American like Grace, who had only been in the country for six months. She wondered what kind of real authority she had to make decisions for someone who already knew the culture and was familiar with the same church teachings.

One morning as the two women got ready to leave their old, frigid apartment in Yokohama, Grace couldn't stand the silence any longer. She asked in her now passable Japanese, "Tell me what you're really feeling. I know you're upset and you're not sharing it."

In response, Sister Yamada still resisted saying anything negative. "Everything's fine. You're doing a great job," she said.

Grace couldn't believe the sister was still resisting so she disagreed and threw back, "I know that's not true. I know that you're not happy. Please tell me what's going on because I can't figure things out on my own."

With their conflict hanging in the air, they looked at each from across the kitchen. Time stood still for a moment as both hesitated to say anything else. Grace had broken through the social etiquette that kept them apart. She was craving honesty and connection. During that moment of silence, she realized that she had been taught in America to speak her truth at any time, and that made her feel authentic. However, she also recognized that Sister Yamada had been taught the opposite: Withhold your opinion or dissenting voice for the good of the group.

Sister Yamada was taking what she considered to be the virtuous road by not contradicting her missionary trainer.

After that difficult conversation, the two women began to discuss their troubles and plans with each other more openly and regularly. Their relationship did not improve overnight, but it evolved incrementally as they learned from each other. Grace was more careful and slower about voicing her opinion whenever and however she wanted to. She became more conscious of the goals of their companionship rather than just considering her own wants, needs, and stresses. On the flip side, Sister Yamada gained more confidence and began sharing her insights and ideas with Grace, rather than following traditional cultural patterns that prevented her from sharing with people in leadership roles.

As you can see in Grace's initially fruitless efforts to work collaboratively with Sister Yamada, when we depend too much on the Avoiding Approach, we do not usually reduce the frequency or intensity of conflict. Of course, we want to avoid unnecessary problems in our relationships and within ourselves, but conflict is a *normal and natural part of life* that we can learn to accept gracefully or begrudgingly.

Most commonly, when we've been hurt and want to avoid further injury, we may choose to prevent conflict situations from occurring in the first place. We might also avoid resolving conflicts in the most important relationships in our lives when they do occur. Both strategies unfortunately prevent cooperative relationships among partners and teams.

Trying to prevent conflict from occurring in the first place can be a noble endeavor, but there is no way to avoid *all* differences that matter between people. We're naturally created and raised as unique beings with distinct temperaments and preferences.

I don't believe that we were created to be the same. We're similar enough to make connections with each other, but our differences can be a great benefit.

We're born with basic human needs that go far beyond the physical necessities of food, clothing, and shelter. We have a deep need to belong to and love others. In other words, we're social creatures who need social connection, but we're often brought into contact with people who disagree with us, even when they love us.

When we avoid sharing who we really are and what we need with other people, we risk feeling like we never really belong. When we avoid resolving the differences between us, we risk our true well-being—physically, emotionally, and spiritually. And when we avoid examining the conflicts within ourselves, we may alienate ourselves from who we really are, putting our mental health and wellness at risk.

From time to time, I've experienced a painful inner conflict that grows worse as I continue to avoid dealing with it. I know from those experiences that there are real dangers in overusing the Avoiding Approach that should not be underestimated, especially in times of social isolation and public turmoil like we've been living through lately.

Putting it simply: To create social connections, we must be vulnerable enough to work through our differences with each other. Respectful conflict resolution—not avoiding it—is at the heart of creating real connections based on the good and bad we see in ourselves and in each other.

What happens when we underuse the Avoiding Approach in conflicts?

Several years ago, while cleaning my daughter Lucie's bedroom, I lay down on my belly on the carpet to look under her bed. Do you know what I found? Countless candy wrappers strewn among old toys, sticks, pens, paper, and everything else that clutters a typical little girl's room. How had she managed to eat that much candy without my knowing? This little sweet tooth had been eating candy behind my back for a very, very long time without my noticing.

I've long had a policy of allowing my kids one major treat a day. I'm rather strict about it because I've wanted my children to grow up healthy and make wise eating choices on a daily basis. With my fifth child, I have to admit that I paid less attention to her sugar intake, but she was still familiar with our house rules about sweets.

As I stared at the evidence of my daughter's rule-breaking, I started to wonder about her character. "What a little cheater!" I thought to myself. "And she's been hiding the evidence for months!"

I needed to talk with the guilty party before convicting her, so I called out, "Hey, Lucie, come here!" My smiling five-year-old came running into her room and looked at me with a bit of mischievousness when she noticed the handful of candy wrappers wadded up in my hand.

"What's this, sweetheart?" I asked her with a serious but gentle tone. Impishly, she looked back at me and simply said, "Candy. I love candy."

"I know you like candy, but this is *a lot* of candy."

She just smiled and probably wondered why I was asking questions when we both already knew she had eaten all the candy. We were in a stalemate because she didn't seem remorseful in the least, and there was clearly no more candy to eat in her room. What next?

"Sweetheart, it's not good for you to be eating this much candy," I told her.

"I know, but I really like it."

I had to hand it to her—she wasn't lying, just stating the facts. Not certain what to do next, I let her leave the room while I pondered how to address her apparent addiction to sugar. What had backfired with my treat policy? Had my rigid rule led to her ignoring it completely?

When we're in positions of authority, we often set and enforce rules. But those who are subject to our rules can decide if they want to keep them or break them. When we're overbearing or competitive, rather than collaborative, people may learn go behind our backs, especially if we refuse to let up and relax occasionally. As I was tossing away Lucie's stash of empty wrappers, I thought about all the Americans who flouted Prohibition, going to speakeasies or making their own moonshine, and I had to laugh. At least she hadn't set up a secret taffy-making operation in her closet!

How does this relate to the Avoiding Approach? We may believe that we're not missing anything by not using the Avoiding Approach very often. We may even be proud of our proactive and confident resolve to face conflicts directly whenever we experience them. We see ourselves as positive, undaunted, and savvy. But how do others see us? Could we sometimes be annoying, petty, or overly taxing? If we *never* avoid conflicts as a tactic, maybe that means we have some blind spots and some missing tools in our conflict resolution skill set.

By under using the Avoiding Approach, especially in appropriate situations, we may be priming ourselves for trouble:

- We may be wasting our time on pointless or insignificant conflicts rather than putting our energies into our most important projects and relationships.

- In our most important relationships, we may be alienating cherished people who have given up on trying to battle us over silly matters that we're committed to addressing, despite their triviality.

- We may also be missing key opportunities to help others save face and preserve their dignity in awkward or tense situations.

- Others may learn to avoid us if we're too confrontational and not attuned to social nuances.

Rather than dismiss the Avoiding Approach as weak or invaluable, we can try to use it with confidence and skill not only to our benefit, but to the benefit of others, especially those we care about. Avoiding has its rightful place alongside Accommodating, Compromising, Competing, and Collaborating, each of which we'll explore in later chapters.

Just as with each of the other five approaches, there are situations in which avoiding will assist us in dealing with conflicts involving contested resources, incompatible roles, and incompatible values. As you learn more about each of the Five Conflict Approaches, you will begin to see how each one comes with specific benefits and drawbacks that flow from the situations in which we choose to use them. Often, we use a variety of approaches over the course of a conflict, especially if it is complex and involves many moving parts, including the ebb and flow of human emotion.

What are the ideal conditions for using the Avoiding Approach in conflict?

Readers, please consider skipping the following introductory story about a threatened sexual assault if this may be triggering to you.

Many years ago, when I was a first-year student in college, my ex-boyfriend, Russell, came looking for me at a play rehearsal. On that night, Russell had some bad intentions. Before Russell arrived, my friends Jen and Kathy rushed into practice to warn me that he had already hit one of my friends, and they begged me to leave rehearsal immediately. Their urging felt rash, but also like the right thing to do. I knew my friends wouldn't lie to me; I began to believe that he might actually try to hurt me too, so I left through a back door.

Once outside and about two blocks away, I could see Russell's lanky frame about 300 feet away striding quickly toward the door of the theater. I had barely missed running into him on my way back to the dorms. "Phew, God is watching out for me," I thought as I hurried up the stairs to my small second-story room.

Within just a few minutes, frustrated that he hadn't found me at my rehearsal, Russell was standing on the sidewalk outside my dorm trying to convince me to come down.

"Come on, Emily, honey. I just want to talk to you," he coaxed.

I refused to go outside because I was now afraid of him—and even if I'd wanted to leave, my dorm mates had locked the door and insisted that I stay put. He finally went home and we breathed a sigh of relief.

A few days later, I began feeling guilty for avoiding him. When Russell asked me to dinner the following weekend, I unwisely agreed to go. "How dangerous could dinner near campus actually be?"

Afterward he suggested that we go to Hepworth Tower, a campus landmark, to wander around. Naively, I said yes and found myself alone with him in a quiet hallway on an empty floor of the building.

In a matter of seconds, he put me in a headlock on the floor. With my face pressed against the thin carpet, I couldn't do anything to fight him. With his overpowering physical strength, he had instantly proved that he was willing and able to hurt me. I was lucky. He had just wanted to scare me, and nothing more happened that night. By the time I made it back to my room and locked the door, shaking with fear, I knew I had no obligation to spend any time with him ever again.

Russell had proven himself unworthy of my trust, and I needed to learn to respect myself enough to avoid that kind of danger again.

Most of us would agree that we should go into avoiding mode in the face of dangers like a predatory ex-boyfriend, but there are many other situations in which we can benefit from using an Avoiding Approach. Take a look at this (not exhaustive) list of situations when avoiding is useful:

1. ***Your well-being is threatened or in danger.***

If you're involved in a potentially dangerous position involving physical violence, emotional abuse, or other forms of harm, you'd do well to avoid further confrontation and flee to safety. Grave consequences result from not realizing that danger can come in the form of a familiar, once-trusted face.

2. ***The conflict issue or the relationship is not important to you.***

You're wise to avoid engaging in the resolution of issues that you care very little about. Why waste your time? If a stranger at Target makes a remark about your kids' bad behavior and you're never going to see them again, maybe you should just avoid that one nasty stranger.

Likewise, at work, there may be a project assignment that kind of annoys you, but you're otherwise happy with the main responsibilities of your job. If you are generally satisfied, you may want to let a small annoyance pass.

Usually, you can tell if you should have avoided a small issue or not by the feelings that arise later. If you soon forget the issue and have moved on, avoiding was a good choice. On the flip side, if you avoided trying to resolve the conflict and bad feelings keep resurfacing, you may need to revise your conflict resolution strategy and address it more directly with a different approach.

There may be situations and relationships that are distant enough that you need to decide how much energy you can realistically put in. Clearly, communicating that you're not interested in resolution may be awkward and painful to the other person, but your honesty allows them to make important decisions to move on with their lives.

3. *There is little or no chance of achieving your goals.*

You may encounter social situations in which you have little opportunity to fulfill your goals, especially when you don't have the power or authority to influence certain outcomes in your favor. Imagine you're trying to get your passport at City Hall and the clerk says you're missing a key signature. You're certainly welcome to complain, but the person at the counter has the power to prevent you from getting your passport in a timely manner. You're more likely to achieve your goals if you avoid confrontation and just spend your energy securing the right signature.

4. *Your main desire is to maintain the status quo.*

When you have little chance of achieving your goals, avoiding helps maintain things the way they currently are, especially if you're comfortable with your routine patterns and resist change. When others advocate new processes and patterns, you may simply avoid responding wholeheartedly to these requests and forge ahead with what brings you balance.

5. *Your main goal is to show respect for and preserve the dignity of another person, and that cannot happen if attempts at compromise or collaboration take place.*

You may want to avoid talking about the elephant in the room if you can tell that the other person would be too embarrassed or maybe even unequipped to have a conversation about that particular elephant. In Western culture, we don't often pay enough attention to face-saving needs, which means that we don't often factor in the need to show respect for those we disagree with.

6. *You're trying to relieve tension in an awkward situation.*

Similar to focusing on face-saving needs for others, you might want to avoid resolving conflict in certain situations because it would be too awkward or uncomfortable for you or the other party.

7. *A complex situation prevents immediate resolution.*

When I mediate, sometimes someone brings up extremely complex issues that are relevant in the grand scheme, but not something relevant to the concerns the parties came to resolve in mediation. While I don't remain silent about the side issues parties bring up, I simply say: "I hear your concern. That is a complex issue that we're not equipped to resolve at this time. Do you mind if we just focus on the matters at hand that brought you to the table?"

8. ***You need to gather more information before making a decision.***

Rather than making a rash decision about how to handle a child's tantrum or respond to a workplace issue that catches you off-guard, take the time to gather the correct information and make a wiser decision.

9. ***You sense that you or the other person need more time to reflect before confronting a conflict.***

The Avoiding Approach allows you and others to reflect before responding to a tense or otherwise undesirable situation. You might be unsure of how to respond effectively, especially when you experience shock, surprise, or other heightened emotions. You demonstrate compassion to yourself and others when you allow for buffer time before trying to resolve issues.

Despite taking some time for reflection, you still need to communicate to the other parties that you're willing and wanting to work out a resolution if you choose to delay. When you avoid a conflict and remain silent, the other party may begin imagining the worst-case scenario. Be kind in demonstrating your willingness to work through hard problems by openly and clearly communicating that you're committed to figuring out a solution (if you are).

Questions for Reflection

1. When do I avoid conflict?

2. How does an Avoiding Approach usually work out for me?

3. In what situations would the Avoiding Approach help me reach my goals or interests?

4. Are there ways I can tweak my avoiding responses to get better results, given the right conditions?

THE AVOIDING APPROACH:

THINGS TO REMEMBER

In conflict resolution based on avoiding, you do not openly seek to satisfy your own needs or the other person's needs.

When and why you might use the Avoiding Approach:

- You might avoid conflict if you believe you have little power to influence outcomes.
- You might have been taught to avoid taboo topics because they are complicated, sensitive, require maturity to discuss, or just create social friction.
- You might use avoidance to be kind and thoughtful to others in awkward or tense situations.
- You may avoid tough topics when you realize that others need a foundation of trust and understanding before they can properly address harder, more personal conflicts.
- You might avoid resolving conflict because you don't care to put the effort into a relationship.
- You might use avoidance if you feel that your well-being is in danger.
- You may also avoid conflict because you don't trust yourself to control your temper or fear that others will lose their tempers and become volatile and/or dangerous.

Benefits:

- You avoid physical, emotional, or other types of danger by avoiding those who might try to harm us, whether intentionally or not.
- You don't waste time in relationships and related conflicts that you don't care enough about to invest in heavily.
- You don't spend your energy on or stress about complex issues that you have little control over.
- You help others feel comfortable and maintain their dignity in your presence despite awkward or tense social situations.
- If you take the time to reflect and cool down before responding, you may create wiser resolutions.

Drawbacks:

- You can miss important windows of opportunity for resolving issues when others are aware of what's going on and invested in finding a solution.
- You may experience the world in a superficial way that prohibits a sense of deep feeling and belonging.
- Important conflict issues do not go away but linger, often returning with greater frequency and intensity. Most people avoid marital, parent-child, and sibling conflict at some point, and it rarely goes away on its own.

Overusing the Avoiding Approach:

- Overdependence on this strategy leads individuals and entire nations into patterns of denial that do not reduce the frequency or intensity of conflict.

- When you avoid sharing who you really are and what you need with other people, you risk feeling like you never truly belong.
- In avoiding the conflict that you experience within yourself, you may alienate yourself from who you truly are and create confusion about what you think and feel.

Underusing the Avoiding Approach:

- You may be wasting your time on pointless or insignificant conflicts rather than putting your energy into your most important projects and relationships.
- In your most important relationships, you may be alienating cherished people who have given up on trying to battle over silly matters that you're committed to addressing despite their triviality.
- You may also be missing key opportunities to help others save face and preserve their dignity in awkward and tense situations.
- Others may learn to avoid you if you're too confrontational and not attuned to social nuances.

Ideal Conditions for the Avoiding Approach:

1. There is danger with real threats to your well-being.
2. The conflict issue or the relationship is not important to you.
3. There is little or no chance of achieving your goals.
4. Your main goal is to maintain the status quo.
5. Your main goal is to show respect for and preserve the dignity of another person and compromise or

collaboration is not possible in the given social situation.

6. You're trying to relieve tension in an awkward situation.

7. A complex situation prevents immediate resolution.

8. You need to gather more information before you make a decision.

9. You sense that you or the other person need more time to reflect before confronting a conflict situation.

Chapter 3

Conflict Approach #2: Accommodating

Growing up in California, I hardly ever went on traditional dates, except to big dances like Homecoming or Prom with boys I knew pretty well. In college, I was often asked out on dates by guys I barely knew for a quick dinner or something low-key like mini golf.

One fall night, I met Tom, a rugged, blond guy, through some mutual friends. I barely knew him, but I accepted his offer to go out that Friday night. Right before picking me up, Tom called to say that we'd be attending a friend's wedding reception in a nearby town. That sounded fine to me, so I happily chatted with him during the car ride and as we walked into the reception hall.

I was not prepared for the warm greeting I got from the bride's parents, who hugged me close and said, "We're so glad that Tom's found such a wonderful girl!" I smiled politely as they congratulated me on dating Tom and finally pieced together the fact that the bride was Tom's ex-long-term girlfriend. Assessing Tom's need to save face in this awkward and painful social situation, I played along with the whole thing because he seemed in desperate need of some social support. While I would have enjoyed a more stress-free evening out with a nice guy, I chose to just roll with the parents' warmth and camaraderie and talked up how great Tom was because the situation seemed to require grace and kindness. You can imagine the look of relief on his face as I leaned into the girlfriend role and avoided shaming him in front of the whole wedding party.

After mingling for an hour or so, Tom suggested that we head home. After we were in the car, he explained the situation and apologized for not warning me ahead of time. We actually had a good laugh about my improv skills.

As a kind gesture, I had accommodated Tom and spared him social pain, but I also wondered what kind of guy would lead me into a lion's den of socially awkward situations with no warning. I had just wanted to have fun with a handsome guy who seemed interested in me, but that's not what our date turned out to be. It wasn't a good start for a new relationship, and we never went out again.

When was the last time you gave up something you wanted so that others could get what they wanted? Did you avoid a fight or some tension because you were willing to sacrifice your idea, the last bite of ice cream, or getting to watch the movie you wanted to see? We often use the word "pleaser" to describe the type of person who gives in and sacrifices themselves to help others get what they want. This is the Accommodating Approach in conflict.

Shortly before I got married, my boss took me aside to have a long conversation about *her* romantic relationship. She told me she was delighted to have a boyfriend who was a pleaser. She mentioned how wonderful it was to have someone who always tried to make things right between them, even when "it wasn't his fault." She said my future husband would be getting the same ideal situation because I was also a pleaser. At the time, I thought she was giving me a back-handed compliment, but it also felt like a warning.

She was right. I am a pleaser at heart. From an early age, I learned the art of accommodating to get what I wanted with the least amount of conflict. Whether at home, church, school, or work, I relied on a limited repertoire of conflict strategies, mostly avoiding and accommodating, to try to meet my needs in conflict situations. I believed that if I could be pleasing and kind enough, I would end up with what I wanted in life: friends, security, love, intimacy, and academic and professional success. I assumed that others would reciprocate my gift of accommodating them in conflict with sacrifices of their own. Of course, that doesn't always happen.

Twenty years ago, to accommodate my new husband, I agreed on a set of plates he chose for our wedding registry that I didn't really like. After capitulating during our short negotiation over what felt, at first, like a small conflict, I resented my weakness for not representing my own interests well enough. Year after year, those plates—such a small issue in the grand scheme of things—reminded me that my tendency to please was not always getting me what I wanted. I could have taken more time to collaborate with my husband but had opted for the familiar, quick, and seemingly less risky approach of accommodating. That choice opened a little chasm in an important relationship in my life.

Until he read this book in an early draft, I don't think my husband knew how much I resented that minor choice as we began our married journey together. It became a symbol of how often I used accommodating as a crutch in all my relationships.

Yet not all accommodating gestures carry the same weight. And we often remember our own sacrifices more than what others have done for us. While I was miffed about the plates, during the next several years, my husband made accommodations for me that had far greater importance than our choice of dinnerware. I recognize that my husband has accommodated me in some of my most important dreams, including having five kids in six short years! In retrospect, it's miraculous that he would agree each time I told him we needed to have another child.

Both at work and at home, you need to be aware that reliance on accommodation can secure peace but can also create deep caverns of resentment and unmet needs if misused (or used chronically). Small conflicts that are inappropriately settled through accommodation can grow bigger and more significant while hidden deep beneath the surface of a relationship.

The Accommodating Approach can easily be overused or misused. We'll learn how to use it purposefully and lovingly in the next few pages, keeping the dangers in mind.

What is the Accommodating Approach?

When we accommodate, we are actively giving in to others' demands. We are addressing others' needs and interests rather than considering our own. Remember that in the Avoiding Approach, we typically don't seek to satisfy anyone else's interests, remaining aloof.

After five long months of searching for a job after the tech industry bubble burst in early 2001, Jeff finally found what seemed like a promising role for him in Washington, D.C. Despite the bureaucratic culture of his new organization, he hoped for the best.

Jeff's boss, Alice, seemed decent at first, but soon demonstrated a nasty streak when criticizing Jeff's work partner, Jennifer, openly during regular staff meetings. Alice kept chipping away at Jennifer's confidence, criticizing her lack of initiative. Jeff kept quiet, hoping to avoid similar treatment by accommodating all his boss's requests, but he couldn't help wondering when he would be on the chopping block.

Shortly after a holiday vacation, Jeff learned from HR that he had messed up a travel request for an upcoming work trip. He had to talk to Alice about the problem—his first real mistake on the job—but he wasn't initially worried about her response because everything had been going fine between them for months.

When he explained the problem and asked for her help, Alice looked Jeff squarely in the face and scolded him loudly for almost fifteen minutes. She finally dismissed him with, "Well, you really screwed yourself, didn't you?!"

Jeff skulked back to his cube and worked out the problem with HR on his own. He tried to dismiss Alice's rampage as an anomaly.

After Jeff returned from his work trip, Alice began focusing her tirades and critiques on him rather than Jennifer. He felt intense pressure and stress because no amount of good work could change his boss's behavior and attitude. Jeff felt trapped in the job because he had a young family to support. He felt that he had to put up with Alice's behavior for their sake.

Eventually, after some counseling, Jeff realized that continually accommodating Alice's bad behavior was not only tearing him down but also allowing her to oppress all the other people in his department. He decided to quit his job, but he didn't quit silently. He met with the executive director of the organization and explained the abuses he and others had endured, recommending that the management team correct the situation.

A year later, Jeff found out that his abusive boss had been officially let go on April Fool's Day. He hadn't wanted to hurt her unnecessarily, but he felt some satisfaction in holding her accountable for her behavior and protecting his colleagues.

Like Jeff, you may feel obligated to accommodate people with power and authority over you. Similar to the related approach of avoiding, accommodating can often be at your own expense. When you accommodate in conflict, you give up something you want and ignore your own interests so that others can achieve theirs.

When and why do people use the Accommodating Approach?

Late one Saturday night, my brother Paul called to share some good news. That night, his son Jake had captured a live tarantula on their driveway, and he knew that my son Aaron would be thrilled.

"Do you want me to bring it over tonight?" Paul asked, eager to share the catch.

You might think I would hesitate about bringing a tarantula into our house, and it's definitely not something I'd choose on my own. But Aaron is a regular teenage biologist who breeds Dubia cockroaches, praying mantises, and pill bugs in the safety of his bedroom/laboratory. Plastic and glass jars filled with desert scorpions, jumping spiders, and exotic plants line the walls. Aaron spends hours observing his creatures, trying to create jungle-like conditions, and I'm happy that he has this passion for science—even though the little beasts creep me out.

I knew that my son had been hoping to find a tarantula all summer. So, when Paul called at 10 p.m. to ask about immediately bringing over the tarantula, I said, "Yes. I'm not going to be home, but I'll let Aaron know."

I didn't see the fuzzy spider arrive, and I have to admit that I avoided Aaron's room for the next couple of weeks, but I'm glad I used the Accommodating Approach in that case.

I accommodate my son's passion and let him bring these creatures into our home because they matter so much to him. This is a case in which he gets what he wants, and I don't—but I don't feel I'm really losing out.

Do you ever agree to something as small as a change in dinner plans or the timing of a staff meeting even though it inconveniences you? Can you do so without feeling like you're on the losing end of the bargain? Are you accommodating in small conflicts, or are you doing so when you actually need to take the time to work out differences with important people through collaboration instead?

Often, our social roles heavily influence who is expected to accommodate whom. For example, in the workplace, employees are generally expected to follow their supervisor's lead, even if that boss is uninformed or misguided. In many cultures, entire populations are expected to accommodate others who have power or social status. Recall how many Japanese people submitted to the will of the emperor and laid down their lives in suicide missions because it was *expected* of them during World War II. Or consider the long history of women catering to men in cultures around the world because their power in society is not equal to men's.

We accommodate others in conflict for a variety of reasons. We're each seeking enough personal power and autonomy to fulfill our needs, wants, and goals. We bump up against others who disagree with us, don't believe us, or simply appear to stand in the way of our achieving our goals and desires, and we react. Often, we use a narrow lens in looking at our relationships, and we think we must be either the master or the servant. We see only two types of responses to conflict: *I will dominate*, or *I will be subservient.* Fortunately, we actually have several responses for effectively handling conflict, depending on the situation at hand.

You might choose to accommodate others to prevent an unnecessary confrontation or to maintain harmony in an awkward or potentially volatile social situation. If your goal is to appear generous or gracious, accommodation is natural. This approach may also preserve others' dignity or your own.

You might accommodate others because you're motivated by fear and a sense of powerlessness rather than altruism. Some negative motivations for accommodating include:

- You fear the hostile reactions of others.

- You feel powerless to get what you want.

- You believe it's expected of you, so you feel obligated.

- You have not learned how to self-advocate.

- You hope others will return the favor, but don't want to risk asking directly.

- You fear being rejected by a person or social group.

Many psychologists emphasize that fear and co-dependency may underlie accommodators' approaches to conflict, but I believe pleasing and accommodation usually involve more complex motivations. Accommodating behavior can be motivated by love, concern, empathy, personal values, optimistic expectations, and positive family culture. Positive motivations include:

- You love and care about the people you're accommodating.

- You empathize with other people's concerns and desires.

- You know that others will return the favor of accommodating.

- You have learned to sacrifice yourself for your family, and this way of life feels most natural and familiar.

- You want to show honor and respect for people in positions of authority.

- You want to demonstrate goodwill toward others.

- You want to set a precedent of generous behavior.

You're probably motivated by a mix of *both* fear and love in accommodation, depending on the situation.

To understand patterns of accommodating others in conflict, let's look at possible benefits and drawbacks of using this approach and ideal conditions for it. As you read, consider which tendencies you display most often.

What are the benefits?

As a new missionary for the Mormon Church in southern Japan, I knew I was in for some unusual social situations. Although my family had often hosted Japanese exchange students at our home in California, after I moved to Japan, I was surprised by unexpected cultural differences. Rather than resist or complain, I learned to go with the flow.

One afternoon, my companion Sister Jenkins and I sat down on tatami mats before a beautifully set luncheon. I enjoyed the delicious and healthy dishes, including miso soup and seaweed salad, until our host brought out the specialty: *basahi*, or raw horsemeat. I had heard about the possibility of being served raw horsemeat, but I was caught off-guard. I had been nearly vegetarian for many years leading up to my missionary service at age 21.

During the preceding few months, I had eaten beef a few times when it was served, but how could I actually take a bite of Seabiscuit or the Black Stallion?

Still, after a moment's hesitation, I graciously accepted a small serving of the horsemeat and smiled politely as I pretended to savor each bite. I understood that the horse meat was not only expensive, but an important social signal of respect and acceptance. I couldn't turn down the offering of friendship if I was truly trying to enter this new culture with openness and gratitude.

Accommodating others often comes with important personal and social rewards, especially in settings where compliance and harmony are expected and rewarded. The benefits of accommodating others in conflict include:

- People tend to rely on you to keep social or work situations running smoothly.

- People may treat you with kindness and accommodation in return.

- You gain a reputation as a considerate, warm person.

- You're complimented on your generosity and likeability.

- You may build group unity by sacrificing personal goals and desires for the benefit of the group.

- You can help maintain a sense of harmony or peace in difficult circumstances.

- You might escape negative attention for dissenting behavior.

Many cultures are founded on principles of accommodation and avoidance to maintain social harmony and homogeneity. Accommodating can bind individuals together in groups that care about and sacrifice for each other. Most societies cannot function properly without some accommodation at home, work, and in the community.

Yet, despite the many potentially positive consequences of an Accommodating Approach, there are drawbacks that relate primarily to overuse or misuse of accommodating.

What are the drawbacks?

When we accommodate others in matters that we actually care about, we may be unknowingly condoning behavior and creating social patterns that hurt us (and others) in the long run. This was the case with the legalization of marijuana in Colorado a few years ago.

Having lived in Colorado for 13 years, I remember the intense PR campaign that brought all kinds of outside influences into the state to convince voters to legalize marijuana in a 2012 referendum. Every public announcement of the vote seemed to emphasize the relative harmlessness of marijuana and the economic benefits of legalizing a drug that many lawmakers themselves had tried at least once or twice during their youth. The message was simple: Don't vote to restrict someone else's right to smoke a joint if they want to. The subtext was also clear: Another person's drug use will never affect a non-user.

Shortly after the first recreational cannabis sales began in January 2014, I regularly encountered dangerous driving situations because other drivers were high. I also began receiving health warnings at the pediatrician's office discussing rising drug use among young people. Unlike alcohol, which also leads to driving deaths and costly addiction, marijuana was not highly regulated when sales began in our state. And there were fewer social norms to guide young adults and adolescents as drug use increased. Drug addiction rates began climbing without adequate community resources to help people work through their addictions.

What we soon discovered was that increased addiction rates *were* affecting regular non-using taxpayers, contrary to the happy-go-lucky 2012 PR campaigns. We were seeing more traffic accidents involving drivers who were high. The increased presence of marijuana in our children's lives demonstrated that legalization was not just about personal drug use—this was a societal choice that all of us had to deal with. The bottom line: Colorado voters' choice to accommodate recreational marijuana as a freely available drug in the state has not really been free for anyone.[10]

Often, as in the case of legalizing marijuana, we don't anticipate all the side effects and drawbacks of accommodating that can lead to increased conflict and complexity. Those drawbacks include:

- You may be taken advantage of by others who see pleasing behavior as weakness.

- You might be condoning destructive or abusive behavior that hurts you as the pleaser and fails to hold the perpetrator of the "bad" behavior accountable.

- You may overuse the approach and fail to please yourself in essential relationships.

- If you use the Accommodating Approach too often, you may generate resentment, which destroys feelings of intimacy and connection with others.

- People may have a hard time getting to know the "real" you behind your self-sacrificing behavior.

- You may not prevent a group spiral into destructive paths if you fail to raise protective boundaries with more assertive approaches.

If you were raised in a family that preferred accommodation in conflict, you're probably familiar with the approach and understand its cues. You may even have confidence that pleasing others will get you where you want to go because you had success with this approach in the past. Maybe friends and colleagues say you're really good with people, and they accommodate you in return for all the kind things you do for them.

But maybe you're not *always* happy with your habit of pleasing others and just don't know other approaches you could try. If that's the case, definitely keep reading!

If you believe your Accommodating Approach is an unchangeable part of your personality, I can tell you from experience that is not the case. You can learn other ways of responding to conflict.

Even if you've been socially rewarded and admired for your ability to use the pleasing approach, you should be aware of some of the dangers.

What happens when we overuse the Accommodating Approach?

When we overuse the Accommodating Approach, we may set ourselves up for dramatic explosions of unmet human need. Like legalizing certain drugs without adequate social protections, overusing accommodating personally or as a society can make us *vulnerable.*

Prior to a mass shooting at Port Arthur in Tasmania in 1996, Australia had relatively lax gun control laws. Without a universal federal policy on guns, the central government accommodated loose and varied gun control laws across its six states and two mainland territories. However, the massacre in 1996 reversed public opinion and motivated state lawmakers to coalesce and create a national firearms policy. With citizen support, lawmakers cooperated to address the issue of gun control, including a nationwide firearms buy-back program, restrictions on ammunition, regulated firearms sales, and the banning of many types of guns.

The horror of the massacre that took the lives of 35 people provided the momentum for citizens and lawmakers to revisit their previous policy of accommodating most people who desired any kind of firearm. As a nation, Australians simply insisted that accommodation of varied, lenient approaches would no longer be tolerated. They decided that what had worked in the past needed to be revisited based on new conditions and shifting societal needs in order to ensure public safety.[11]

As the Australian government's move from loosely organized accommodating to a more unified firearms policy demonstrates, societal needs change over time, demanding new conflict approaches. As a society, citizens and officials chose to revisit the issue with a different approach to address safety needs and a changing social landscape in Australia. The same kind of shifts can happen on a smaller scale in organizations and families.

If you are overusing the accommodation approach on a personal level, many of your important needs may not be met because you're giving in to what others want or expect of you without respecting your own needs and wants. You may feel deep resentment toward and alienation from those who expect you to accommodate them regularly, especially those who use power, influence, or manipulation to get you to step in line with their wishes. You may be hoping that someone will notice how kind and generous you are when there is a disagreement. But if you're working with people who are highly competitive, they may not notice, appreciate, or understand your "sacrifices" on their behalf. They may wonder why you don't care as much as they do about the outcomes of particular conflicts. Why do you just give in every time?

As I've gotten older, I've realized that continually accommodating others in conflict is like trying to stay underwater: You only have so much lung capacity until you need to come up for a deep breath, only to submerge yourself again. Perhaps you've experienced this "underwater" feeling when you've had difficult house guests for too long. Or maybe you've held your tongue in a team meeting week after week only to find yourself exploding one day at the smallest provocation.

When we expand our conflict repertoire, we not only breathe easier, but allow others to do the same.

I want to mention the most serious result of overusing accommodation in conflict, which is "obliger fatigue." This term refers to an extreme version of the explosion at a team meeting I mentioned above. When you accommodate or please others constantly, you may experience a buildup of tension that leads you to blow up and say: "No more!"

As Dr. Marshall Rosenberg, author of *Nonviolent Communication: A Language of Life*, says, "Anger is an alarm clock for an unmet need." If you are experiencing obliger fatigue from over-accommodating others, I can tell you that your exhaustion, anger, or distress could call for more expansive and diverse approaches to conflict in your life.

What happens when we underuse the Accommodating Approach?

I can be pretty stubborn about when and how I accommodate others. For example, I found it easy to accommodate the requests and needs of the Japanese people I taught as a missionary, but I had a harder time accommodating the requests of fellow missionaries because I expected different responses from them.

Near the end of my mission in the early 1990s, my Japanese friends invited me to parties and outings to make sure I took advantage of all Japan had to offer before I returned to the United States. We visited famous shrines and ate delicious food, but I have to admit that I thought it was mostly a waste of time. Missionaries usually work in pairs, so I suggested that my partner and I split up so she could keep working while I attended the obligatory parties with my friends.

I assumed my companion was on board with this arrangement and felt the same way about the parties until one afternoon when she exploded at me, "Why don't you want me with you at all these special events?"

"It's not that I don't want you with me," I countered, taken aback by her angry tone, "I thought you would want to be doing real work rather than just playing around with people that I've known for a long time that you haven't."

"It's important that we do things *together;* that we matter to each other," she explained. "I thought we were friends. When did I ever say that I didn't want to go with you?"

I realized that I hadn't ever asked her opinion. I had just expected her to trust and accommodate me in my plan to keep up our missionary work. Through our conversation, I realized that she was now asking me to accommodate her request to work together rather than apart. In all my focus on accommodating my Japanese friends, I had not thought about truly considering or accommodating her needs.

From this experience, I realized how important it is to understand not only *why* you're accommodating others but *whom* you're accommodating. I needed to learn that my missionary companion had important needs that I should pay attention to, which might be even more important than the needs of the other people we were working with at the time.

The experience in Japan influenced how I now treat my spouse and children. I need to constantly remind myself that those closest to me have needs that I should accommodate and treat with at least as much respect as the needs of people outside of our home.

Beware: If you're underusing the accommodation approach in favor of more aggressive approaches, you may be getting your way more than you should. You may be competitively using your power to influence conflict outcomes in your favor without paying attention to the needs of others. While you might think you're the one "winning" in your conflicts, you may be deepening resentment in those you are "beating" in conflict situations.

If you're rarely accommodating others in your most important relationships, you could be missing out on key opportunities to demonstrate love and respect for those you care about. Those who accommodate you in conflict regularly may be secretly hoping you will someday return the favor of their accommodation. When you fail to reciprocate their extension of goodwill and self-sacrifice, over time, the intimacy, love, and trust you once experienced could diminish.

As I deepen my understanding of conflict, I'm realizing that in trying to course correct my "pleaser" tendencies, I may have begun *underusing* the Accommodating Approach. In fact, in my most secure relationships, I've become much more demanding and directly request what I need.

I've noticed that when working remotely in my home office, I often pick up my cell phone and call my children with requests, such as, "Please get your piano practice done now," or "Have you mowed the lawn yet?" or "Please wake up your brother because it's 10 a.m."

In all my attempts to demonstrate confidence and leadership, I probably come across as domineering and less empathetic than I used to, and I worry about that. All of us can get caught up in overcorrecting the otherwise kind and thoughtful behavior that once led us to always accommodate others in our lives.

Pay close attention to the interplay between competitors and accommodators in relation to underusing and overusing the Accommodating Approach. There are some well-worn patterns between individuals who use this approach and whose relationships are co-dependent and toxic. In many cultures, women are expected to accommodate men regularly and even wait to eat until all the men and boys in the family have finished their meals. In many of these same cultures, women and girls have less access to healthcare and education, so they become more vulnerable to disease and the general effects of poverty. For centuries, entire cultures have been centered on women and girls accommodating men in nearly every social situation.

In Western cultures, generally speaking, young people hold more power and influence than aging adults. For example, rather than respecting grandma's wishes to remain in her own home, adult children will make the ultimate decision to move her into a nursing home.

When cultural patterns of competition and accommodation become too rigid, we miss out on the deep connection and understanding between women and men, girls and boys, and old and young.

What are the ideal conditions for using the Accommodating Approach?

Like you, my everyday life involves a series of accommodations that help me create balance among a lot of different activities—parenting, working part-time, and volunteering for several organizations. On a typical workday, I wake up by 7 a.m. to make sure my kids have eaten and prepared themselves for school. After I drop off the kids with one of my two carpools, I take the dog for a hike in the mountains, then hurry back to shower and get dressed for work.

From about 10 a.m. to 3 p.m. (with a quick carpool run around 1:30 p.m. to one of two elementary schools), I carry out my regular job for a university while my puppy sleeps on the couch beside me. My husband may check in with me for a quick call to talk about our day.

Around 3 p.m., I emerge from my home office and check on the kids and their various activities. I may begin dinner and usually encourage the kids to practice their musical instruments and get some exercise. On my best days, I begin assembling a plan for dinner that involves help from one of the kids on a rotating basis.

Around 5:30 p.m., we usually eat together, then spread out to do homework and work on projects. I may throw some laundry into the washer in between responding to texts and scheduling a hike with friends for the end of the week.

From 7 to 9 p.m., I work on writing projects, respond to emails or do volunteer assignments. By 9 p.m., I gather the family for prayer before separating off for a good night talk with each of my five children. Finishing around 10 p.m., I wander down the stairs to check on my husband before deciding whether to go to bed or work a little longer.

In my world, this schedule of many accommodations for others allows me to mother and work in ways that bring fulfillment and purpose to my life. I regularly shift focus to different people and activities, but this shifting brings the adventure, diversity, and opportunities that make my life meaningful and rich.

Like any of the Five Conflict Approaches, we can underuse or overuse accommodating. Some of the most ideal conditions for using it well include moments when:

1. *There is not much chance of achieving your interests.*

Remember Alice and Jeff? When interacting with a boss like Alice, Jeff knew he had little power to change his workplace environment and his boss's treatment of him and his coworkers. When Alice doled out work assignments, Jeff usually just accepted his responsibilities and went with the flow. Until he was ready to leave for another job, he accommodated her to preserve his sanity and livelihood and to get through each day without too much stress.

2. *The outcomes of this particular conflict are not important to you.*

When you're not concerned about the outcome of a decision, it makes sense to accommodate. If your date prefers Chinese food and you don't care, why not accommodate him or her? You don't have to make a big deal out of something when the stakes are low for you.

3. *You believe that satisfying your interests will in some way alter or damage a relationship that you care about.*

Will speaking up to defend your opinions or advocate for your ideas rile a cantankerous person who has sway over a person or group you care about? Even as a small girl, I remember steering clear of my two grandfathers when they lived with us temporarily (at different times) because I wanted our home to be as peaceful as possible despite their ornery tempers and idiosyncrasies. I tried to "behave" and accommodate them so that my family would have more peace.

4. *Your highest priority is to demonstrate that you are a kind and generous person.*

I've played roles in my life—including missionary, schoolteacher, and mediator—that have led me to accommodate others in order to demonstrate my goodwill and affirm my identity as a kind and generous person. Many customer service roles demand this kind of full accommodation to others, no matter what our personal feelings might be.

If you are a regular accommodator and are experiencing some of the drawbacks of overuse or misuse of this approach, you can begin experimenting with new approaches such as compromising, competing, and collaborating to build stronger, more authentic relationships with others. In meeting conflicts with a full tool belt of responses, you'll find more personal satisfaction and greater connection with family, friends, and coworkers.

Likewise, if you regularly interact with someone who accommodates you and others too frequently, you can help that person explore new possibilities. You may be the motivation or the positive nudge that will help a chronic accommodator develop greater intimacy and trust. Those you love can learn to express their true needs and desires in productive ways, rather than using a mask that says, "I don't need you or anything." You'll both experience aches and pains, as well as moments when you don't know what to do, but the efforts you make together will be worth it.

Questions for Reflection

1. When do I accommodate others in conflict?

2. What kinds of outcomes do I expect when I use this approach?

3. What kinds of outcomes do I usually achieve when I accommodate?

4. Are there situations in my life when I am accommodating too much or too little?

5. If I'm accommodating too much or too little, what other approach would be more effective?

THE ACCOMMODATING APPROACH:

THINGS TO REMEMBER

In conflict resolution based on accommodating, you give up something you want and ignore your own interests so that others can achieve their goals.

When and why you might use the Accommodating Approach:

- You may accommodate others if you are expected to, especially in certain social roles.
- You may use accommodation to prevent an unnecessary confrontation or to maintain harmony in an awkward or potentially volatile social situation.
- You might accommodate others to appear generous or gracious.
- You might accommodate to preserve your own and others' dignity as a sign of your gracious nature and identity.
- You may use accommodation as a sign of deference to an authority figure or a person with more power.
- You may accommodate others because you're motivated by fear and a sense of powerlessness.

Benefits:

- People tend to rely on you.
- People may treat you with kindness in return.

- You gain a reputation as a considerate, easy-going person.
- You're complimented on your generosity and likeability.
- You build group unity by sacrificing personal goals and desires for the benefit of the group.
- You may help maintain a sense of harmony or peace in relationships.
- You may escape negative attention or notice for dissenting behavior because accommodating is required in certain social settings.

Drawbacks:

- You may be taken advantage of by others who see pleasing behavior as weakness.
- You may fail to meet your needs in essential relationships.
- You may generate resentment, which destroys feelings of intimacy and connection with others.
- People may have a hard time getting to know the real you behind your self-sacrificing behavior.
- You may be condoning destructive or abusive behavior.
- You may fail to prevent a group from spiraling into destructive paths (codependent/toxic)

Overusing the Accommodating Approach:

- Many of your important needs may not be met because you're giving in to what others want or expect of you without respecting your own needs and wants.
- You may feel deep resentment toward and alienation from those who expect you to accommodate

them regularly, especially those who use power, influence, or manipulation to get you to step in line with their wishes.

- One of the most serious results of overusing accommodation in conflict is obliger fatigue. This term refers to those who accommodate or please others too much in conflict and who experience a buildup that leads to a crisis or "blowing up."

Underusing the Accommodating Approach:

- If you're underusing the accommodation approach in favor of more aggressive approaches, you may be getting your way more than you should.
- While you may think that you're the one "winning" in conflicts, you may actually be deepening resentment in those you're "beating" in conflict situations.
- If you're rarely accommodating others in your most important relationships, you may be missing out on opportunities to demonstrate love and respect for those you care about.

Ideal Conditions for the Accommodating Approach:

1. There is not much chance of achieving your interests.
2. The outcomes of this particular conflict are not important to you.
3. You believe that satisfying your interests will in some way alter or damage a relationship that you care about.
4. Your highest priority is to demonstrate that you are a kind and generous person.

Chapter 4

Conflict Approach #3: Compromising

Back in June 2020, my beloved Brittany spaniel Maisie was hit by a car. I mourned her loss but soon longed for another Brittany spaniel. My husband was not excited. He wanted to focus on getting our new yard set up without worrying about building a fence for another high-energy dog like Maisie.

A few months after I had first suggested a new dog, I again approached my husband, but this time I had a compromise position. "Ken, Could we get this little Cockalier puppy advertised online? These guys are known to be friendly to strangers, low shed, *moderate* energy, very teachable, and unlikely to run away. What do you think?"

This time I could tell I had some traction! Ken seemed open to the idea, so I pulled up a picture of a cute, fuzzy blonde dog that fit within our budget. I agreed to be the primary caregiver (as I was with Maisie) and to never let the dog sleep on our bed, which Ken detests.

That same day, my daughter and I drove to a nearby town to take a look at Mr. Darcy, the darling Cockalier. It was love at first sight, and he soon became part of our family. Yes, I am the one who takes the dog out on walks every day. I shoo him off the couch and our bed to keep my husband happy with our deal. Mr. Darcy isn't the Brittany I originally wanted, but he fits the bill as the awesome canine companion I was looking for. A perfect compromise.

Most of us are familiar with simple compromises, like getting a dog the whole family likes or following traffic laws and regulations, even though we'd like to speed through a red light or park wherever we want. We restrain ourselves; we work through social situations without a hassle in a fair and equitable way.

For example, if you negotiate to buy a house, you'll often begin with a low offer and expect the seller to counter with a higher number. You allow for this because you assume that you'll meet somewhere in the middle after some haggling. Compromise may include some game-playing, but it may also represent honest efforts to place some value on other people's goals while simultaneously respecting your own.

In Western society, we often compromise quickly to deal with conflicts and avoid damaging our social relationships too much. Despite how frequently we use it, compromise does not always help us. In some cases, it's easy to meet in the middle—especially where money is concerned. But compromise gets harder when deciding who gets to speak for how long or how to divide undesirable job responsibilities at work.

It's easy to understand the process of compromise, or "splitting the difference." But have you ever agreed on a deal too quickly and later realized that you are only getting partial satisfaction? In our hurry to end conflicts, sometimes we act too hastily and agree to bad terms. We may choose to "meet in the middle" when the middle is not a good place to be. Remember the story of King Solomon's testing of two mothers who claimed ownership of the same baby? He suggested they compromise by cutting the baby in half. Compromising can lead to more conflict in the future if the compromise doesn't address the larger underlying issues.

Let's discuss how, when, and why we compromise, and how to benefit most with this approach.

What is the Compromising Approach?

The need for compromise goes well beyond deciding whether to get a dog or if the pet can sleep on your bed— although those issues matter to me personally. When it comes to complex political and social issues, compromise is critical for getting traction when full collaboration is less likely.

In 2003, Mitt Romney became the Republican governor of Massachusetts with a predominantly Democratic state legislature—a situation ripe for compromise. Governor Romney publicly declared his interest in securing healthcare coverage for all (or nearly all) Massachusettsans. He wanted to fix the entire system but had to garner support from a wide variety of constituents and interests, including Libertarians, the Massachusetts Taxpayers Foundation, and sceptics from liberal institutions who were already committed to addressing the issue in principle.

As a conservative politician, Romney refused to support an employer tax to fund the uninsured but instead chose to build a strong partnership with Massachusetts Senator Ted Kennedy to create new options. Together, they sought to build a broad coalition of healthcare, labor, and religious groups who weighed in with ideas about what eventually became known as "Romneycare."

Rather than raise the employer tax, state lawmakers decided to increase the cigarette tax, channel federal grants into the healthcare program, and use money from individual and employer penalties to fund the program. Despite recurring tensions, the diverse interests managed to craft a workable plan for the state of Massachusetts with only a few parties (such as small business owners) expressing some dissatisfaction.

From start to finish, politicians and stakeholders jockeyed for ways to fund insurance coverage with Governor Romney's emphasis on finding a viable, if not perfect, solution. At the onset he stated, "Let's not let perfection be the enemy of the good. Let's get something out there that moves us forward. We're all speaking from the same book." Romney vetoed several of the legislative branch's additions to the bill, but in the end, more than 98 percent of Massachusetts citizens had health insurance.[12]

When we use the Compromising Approach, each party settles for partial satisfaction of what they want by giving up something. This approach usually helps us maintain the stability of our social relationships. In Western culture, compromise is a common approach to everyday conflict with both strangers and those we know well. But in some situations, compromising is considered a lose-lose strategy, because no party leaves with everything they wanted in the first place.

A helpful visual for seeing the problem with taking the quickest Compromising Approach is two people who want to use the same orange in a recipe. One wants to grate the peel to get the zest. The other wants the fruit inside. If they rush to compromise, they may split the orange in half, giving each person half of the fruit inside and half of the peel. If they discuss their needs first, they'll create a viable plan in which each gets most of what they really want.

Misusing the Compromising Approach is also possible to in trying to settle disputes over fairness and social privileges that need a more comprehensive approach such as collaborating, which we will discuss in the next chapter.

When and why do people use the Compromising Approach?

When we have serious values differences, limited time, and full collaboration is not possible, we often turn to compromise. But can you really compromise on key issues that reflect core values integral to your identity?

In 2015, when the U.S. Supreme Court ruled that all U.S. states must allow same-sex marriage, the state of Utah took preemptive legislative action to prepare for this legal change. Rather than wait for future court cases to resolve questions about the ruling and produce real winners and losers, the Utah State legislature brought key stakeholders, including Equality Utah and The Church of Jesus Christ of Latter-day Saints, to the negotiating table.

Contrary to common practice, instead of crafting legislation to protect one population over another, the Utah state legislature set to work to secure much-needed protections for the LGBTQ+ *and* religious communities. Gathering all stakeholders together, the legislators created a two-bill package that would protect the LGBTQ+ community from discrimination in housing and hiring while securing religious freedom protections for religious entities and individuals. Signaling the role of compromise in drafting these bills, the parties agreed to leave public accommodations issues off the table because they are so difficult to legislate.

Commenting on the power of simultaneously securing protections for these two different constituencies, Senator J. Stuart Adams shared:

In the end, none of the stakeholders got everything they wanted, but everyone gained specific and very significant statutory protections that a court could not deliver, and all without the rancor experienced elsewhere. The result is a less costly, more enforceable, and more decent legal regime in which all can coexist, true to who we are while respecting others for who they are.

—Sen. J. Stuart Adams,
"*Cultivating Common Ground: Lessons from Utah for Living with our Differences*" (2018)[13]

Despite real and perceived value differences as illustrated in what became known as the Utah Compromise, we can make progress and move toward our ultimate goals in a paced and phased way through compromise without abandoning critical features of our identities.

Outside the political sphere, we all use the Compromising Approach in many ways. Compromising helps us settle conflicts quickly in socially acceptable ways, like splitting the last cookie in half when two people both want it. Every day, we make small sacrifices for others, expecting they'll return the favor. We hope that giving up some things we want will help us work through the disagreements and differences in our lives at home and at work.

Some of us get really anxious when we have to deal with conflict. In our anxiety, we may want the conflict to be over ASAP, so we make compromising offers that don't really resolve the main issues of the conflict. An example of this is agreeing to cut off strong friendships with your guy friends because your boyfriend gets jealous, and you don't want him to worry about your loyalty. This type of compromise does not truly resolve central issues in your relationship and creates further conflict down the road.

Like accommodation, compromise lies along the scale of giving others what they want in conflict. While we give up *everything* we want in accommodation, in compromise, we give up large and small things—and expect the other party to do the same—in order to quickly resolve issues that are really more complex than we'd like to admit.

Too often we ride the wave of anxiety conflict can create and choose fast results over good results. Unsettled by the conflict, we offer up personal sacrifices that indulge others and ultimately represent our weakness in facing up to difficult or annoying situations. In the Utah Compromise, legislators had a short legislative period for negotiating differences, but they remained committed to addressing the primary concerns of all the main stakeholders. Despite criticism from without and within, they didn't bend away from their central purpose until the bills passed.

In my early parenting days, I remember the stress I associated with checking out at Walmart with several small children in tow. The store had placed Matchbox cars on a bottom shelf, so every time we walked down a particular aisle, I had to negotiate with my car-obsessed two-year-old boy about whether or not he could buy a toy car. Sometimes, I just couldn't say no because he put up such a fuss and cried so loudly, and I would buy him a colorful car if he promised to stop crying. While I enjoyed the momentary quiet that I bought with one small Matchbox car, I had created the expectation that each time we walked into Walmart we would walk out with a new mini Corvette or Jeep. My compromise did not benefit either of us in the long run but reflected my emotional fatigue as a young, worn out mother of toddlers.

At times, we may choose to compromise because we're actually pressed for time and need to make a quick decision while still providing an air of fairness and respect for the relationship. For example, when two students show up at the same time in my office to seek advice and counsel about a conflict, I have to triage my time and attention. If I'm the only person in the office, I may ask one student to wait for 10 to 15 minutes or schedule another time for the student to come back. Usually, there is no way for me to accommodate both at the same time due to the confidential nature of our work together.

If you're in a similar situation, you might be aware that you need to create the reality and appearance of fairness among disputing parties and set a just and fair precedent for any future conflicts. If you're in a position of authority, you build trust with those you serve by making fair compromises that don't favor one party over another. Likewise, when you perceive resistance from people who have equal power to influence outcomes, you'll often seek a compromise because it's better than no decision at all.

Compromise can help us avoid tricky situations that reflect the needs of more than one person. For example, if I enter a social situation where I'm not comfortable, I can signal to my husband that we need to leave sooner than he had intended. We cover for each other and adjust according to each of our needs and desires. Because we value our relationship, we keep communicating and adjusting with each new compromising decision.

Finally, when we compromise, we show our self-confidence while still respecting others' goals and interests. Rather than agreeing to go to a restaurant I dislike, I make a counter suggestion that represents my needs and my dinner partner's. Negotiation takes skill and practice, plus a dose of self-confidence. In many respects, making compromising offers reflects an understanding that you're not the only one responsible for a conflict situation—that's why both people need to make some sacrifices to resolve it.

Rather than seeing compromise as a sign of weakness or strength, I usually suggest to my clients that they focus more on *benefits and drawbacks*—in other words, when compromise *makes sense* and when it does not.

What are the potential benefits?

Like most couples, my husband and I often need to compromise about our travel plans. We both love tropical adventures, but my husband dislikes visiting most museums and historical sites, which I adore. As part of an extended German family that meets every two years for reunions in Europe, I often yearn to join my family in interesting cultural settings.

I'm also an avid genealogist who loves to collect historical information in archives in far-flung villages. This is exciting and stimulating, like a grand treasure hunt. For Ken, rummaging through an archive is pure torture. But we do like spending time with each other on vacation and try to include travel together in our family budget. We have even created bucket list travel plans as a couple and with our children to guide our choices.

A few years ago, we were invited to attend my Schweinitz family reunion in Poland. I longed for our family to attend together. This type of event held a special place on my personal bucket list of adventures that I wanted to share with my children, but I knew that traveling to Europe would cost a fortune for our entire family. Considering our financial constraints and divergent travel priorities, I wondered how to approach Ken about the trip. I knew he would rather go adventuring in the Caribbean or Pacific that year. Going alone would mean some awkward extended family moments for me, lonely nights, and no one to create memories with me in a place that I love.

"Honey, I really want to us to attend the family reunion in Poland this summer. What do you think?"

"Europe's super expensive in the summer, and I definitely don't want to go. What about the kids? Who's going to take care of them?"

"We can figure it out," I said cautiously. "I just don't want you to be sad if I go by myself. It's kind of a once-in-a-lifetime chance to meet some of my relatives and learn more family history."

He seemed to be paying attention to what the opportunity meant to me, so I began to explain my idea, "We can do a getaway just for the two of us in the fall, but how about if I go on my own to Poland and do all my genealogy stuff, then meet up with my mom at the reunion?"

"I don't want to make separate vacations a regular thing, but if you want to go this time and make arrangements for the kids, I know we can figure it out."

I knew I could have convinced Ken to come with me, but he wouldn't have enjoyed it nearly as much as a more athletic vacation later on. I've realized that it's okay not to have the same passions as your spouse or close friends. The solo trip let me explore in a way that filled my soul. I compromised up front by going on my own, so that I wouldn't have to compromise throughout the entire trip. By the end of my time in Poland, I was ready for some steady human company, but I appreciated the opportunity to adventure on my own terms.

Within a couple of years, extended family members organized a more affordable and domestic Schweinitz reunion in Pennsylvania where our first ancestors had settled. This more affordable option ultimately satisfied my need for my children to get to know their German relatives and roots while preserving our bank account!

If you can avoid the game playing that comes with compromise, you may arrive at some workable solutions in daily situations. Some benefits of compromising in conflict include:

- Compromise is generally considered fast and efficient.

- This approach is easily understood and applied by others in Western culture.

- With compromise, conflict is removed while relationships are maintained.

- Compromise is considered an acceptable way of dealing with conflict in many cultures

Generally, compromise is understood and often expected in Western cultures. However, there are drawbacks, especially in situations where power between the parties is unequal.

What are the drawbacks?

You already know that I love to travel, so I'll tell you another story about travel and compromise. As Thanksgiving drew close a few years ago when we had just three little kids, I felt sad about missing out on seeing my aunts, uncles, and cousins at my side of the family's biggest holiday get-together. After moving to Colorado, my husband and I spent nearly every major holiday with his family (my in-laws) who lived close by in Denver. I enjoyed celebrating with his family, but I couldn't help but long to join my family's pre-dinner walk in the California hills and listen to the crooning of folk tunes accompanied by my cousin's guitar.

I wondered how I could participate in my family's California Thanksgiving festivities while staying within our budget and making sure my in-laws knew that I cared about them.

"How about I take Aaron and Lucie with me to California while you stay here with George in Colorado?"

Ken just stared at me and wondered why I would come up with such a crazy plan during a family holiday. This was definitely not my husband's first choice, but he thought about it for a moment and said, "How's that going to work? Are you sure?"

Used to my schemes, Ken gave me some space to figure things out, and we ended up going with my original plan. Assuming that this would somehow satisfy both our wishes and the wishes of our respective family members in Colorado and California, we split up our nuclear family. I set off on the airplane with two small children, a large double stroller, and too much luggage.

I enjoyed seeing my family in California, but during the entire holiday weekend, I felt so strange being separated from my husband and George. I wondered how I could feel truly connected with family during this important holiday when I had left two of the most important people in my life behind.

When I returned home, I admitted to Ken how lonely I had been without him and our oldest son in California. He just looked at me and said, "I felt the same. I thought you would be lonely, but I knew that you weren't going to back down easily and needed to experience it for yourself."

At that point in my life, this compromise failed to provide the sense of connection and belonging I was originally seeking. Yet, my decision did provide some insight into how my values and priorities had changed and instilled in me an even greater desire to keep my nuclear family together, especially during the holidays.

As you can see in my divide-and-conquer Thanksgiving debacle, using compromise inappropriately and too frequently in situations that demand greater collaboration may result in negative results:

- Each party in a conflict might give up something to resolve the conflict (lose-lose, in that sense).

- Compromise may not provide us with what we desire—we usually get only part of what we want. When only a portion of our interests are satisfied, our solution may actually perpetuate our problems.

- Compromise decisions may require close monitoring and control to ensure that everyone follows through with what they agreed to.

- Some decisions may not work if people ask for too much in the beginning.

- This approach does not usually contribute to building trust in the long run.

- Compromise may reflect an inability to connect on a deeper level over difficult issues, masking greater conflicts that need true resolution.

- When we compromise too much and too quickly in our important intimate relationships, we may be missing out on important opportunities to collaborate and dig deeper into each other's needs, desires, and expectations.

- If we compromise without thoughtful reflection, we may be disregarding some of our important values and long-term objectives, which could leave us in a worse position than when we started.

Be cautious about compromising important values and beliefs too easily when resolving conflicts. If you do, you'll create *internal conflict*, which rarely leads to more peace. While compromising our values and beliefs can cause serious damage to our sense of self, we also need to recognize that compromise is an absolute must in certain areas, including politics. I may disagree strongly with a politician's stance on one particular issue, such as abortion, climate change, the death penalty, the right to bear arms, and so on, but I have to balance my decisions as a voter based on my assessment of the overall character and actions of the individuals on the ballot. We must be wary of using one policy as a litmus test if the government responsibilities of the candidate are vast and changing.

We put ourselves in jeopardy of supporting figureheads, rather than actual human beings who will make decisions contrary to our overall values, if we only vote according to one or a few hot-button policies. Compromise in policymaking is a given and reflects the nature of the process, but compromise with our character assessments of politicians may be dangerous.

What happens when we overuse the Compromising Approach?

You may have experienced that deep ache that comes with compromising your deepest values and long-term objectives because you think it will get you what you really want, like love or job success. If we compromise our core values, we create inner turmoil that is not sustainable.

My friend Jocelyn told me about a significant mistake she made compromising her standards of honesty as a college student traveling in Europe. She had been enjoying the sites as a tourist one day and didn't imagine she'd encounter an ethical dilemma as she left the metro station.

Jocelyn and her boyfriend had just exited their subway car before passing through the ticket checkpoint. Rather than purchase additional tickets for the next leg of the journey, Jason said, "Just jump over it. No one will see you, and we'll have more money to spend on other stuff."

"What?" Jocelyn couldn't quite believe what Jason had said. She'd *never* not paid for a transportation ticket on purpose. That seemed silly to even contemplate, but Jason's urging made her actually consider it. Before she could think twice, he was jumping over the exit gate, and she was following him as quickly as she could.

Within 30 seconds, they were approached by a stern-faced policeman who ordered them to follow him and pay a significant fine, far beyond the normal ticket price. Jocelyn felt not only public shame but a sense of serious disappointment in herself. How could she have thrown out her long-standing personal value of honesty in a matter of seconds?

In the end, Jocelyn disliked herself for the compromise she made and felt greater distance from her boyfriend.

I share Jocelyn's story to demonstrate that compromising your values and standards comes at a high price. Trust yourself in those moments of ethical decision making. Sticking to your core values leads to greater confidence and personal peace.

If you over-compromise like Jocelyn did, you'll probably experience resentment that feels like "buyer's remorse." It's that feeling you have when you've paid too high of a price for the compromise resolution you agreed to. Because compromise usually involves giving up some part of what you want to reach an agreement, be careful not to overuse it in conflicts involving your core needs and fundamental values and beliefs.

Beware of creating an internal imbalance that is not sustainable.

A chronic compromiser delivers quick solutions and comes across as playing games. People who overuse compromise often seem hard to get close to. Chronic compromisers avoid discussions about the real issues they face, the "hard" stuff that requires vulnerability. Rather than invest in collaborating with others about deep concerns, they overuse compromise to get through conflicts quickly and efficiently in the moment, but not necessarily in the long run.

I've known people who've overused compromise to bypass important issues until they reach a point where they realize they need real understanding and collaboration. They've been so quick to give up their own needs and point of view to speed through conflict that they've lost out on key opportunities to build unity and connection with those they care about.

As a church volunteer, I hated organizing events with my acquaintance Janet because our differences of opinion often became emotionally charged. She just seemed to push my buttons. Even her tone of voice and word choices annoyed me, so I tried to resolve our differences as quickly as possible, like a haggle in a marketplace. I focused purely on compromise rather than collaboration to speed through my dealings with her.

When our volunteer time came to an end, I realized that I had not developed a strong relationship with Janet as had other colleagues who had been more patient and understanding of her personality. While I recognize that most of us are not going to grow close to *everyone* we work with, my over-reliance on quick, easy compromises with Janet created an unnecessary barrier between us and prohibited a friendship that might have blossomed with greater care.

We all want to seem flexible in key conflict situations in our lives. However, when we are quick to compromise every time, this can indicate inability or discomfort with showing who we really are and increase our loneliness and sense of alienation.

Are you scared to let others know how you really think and feel? Be wary of using compromise too quickly and frequently if you are not experiencing a sense of belonging and attachment with others in your life. You need human connection to other fellow travelers on this often rigorous life journey.

What happens when we underuse the Compromising Approach?

Sometimes we refuse to compromise with others because we think it will be a sign of weakness. I've often found myself trapped in this type of thinking because I'm used to having some control over other people's life choices. We can definitely abuse our positions of power and refuse to compromise, even when it makes the most sense.

Several years ago, I realized how my control over my children had transformed into a refusal to compromise at times. For example, my young daughter often ignored the time we set aside for music practice in our house. I struggled on a daily basis to find the right words to get her to practice her violin.

How could I explain to her how sick and tired I was of nagging her to practice? The Suzuki violin method demanded a lot of me as a parent, and I wasn't about to watch all our (my) effort go to waste, so I felt justified in demanding that she practice. One particular day (among many), she wasn't having it.

"No, I don't want to. You can't make me do it."

She was right. I couldn't actually *make* her draw the bow across the strings. What was I going to do?

I took a break from the standoff and realized that all my demanding over the years had led to an impasse that my parenting authority couldn't overcome. My other kids were waiting for my attention, and I only had so much energy to put into this battle. Rather than compete endlessly for a "win" over violin practice, I realized that some compromise was needed.

Eventually, after many long talks, my daughter and I created a plan for her to continue with orchestra but drop the private lessons she disliked for a little while. Rather than seeking ultimate victory, I compromised, which led to more violin playing and less whining in the long run.

Some of us underuse compromise when resolving conflict because we're afraid to speak up and would rather accommodate or avoid others in conflict. Have you ever said, "Whatever you want to do is fine," when you actually *do* care and "whatever" isn't really fine? Carefully consider the reasons why you are not sharing what you want and need, especially with those you care about.

If you have too little social power and hardly any compromise in your life, you may be using avoiding and accommodating too often. Compromise represents a more balanced approach than merely trying to avoid issues altogether. A way to transition toward more compromise is to imagine *counter offers* you could make to loved ones or a boss. Instead of saying, "I'm sick of doing what you want me to do all the time," could you follow my daughter's lead and say something like, "I'll practice my orchestra music if I don't have to take lessons every week?"

Compromise allows you to balance out everyone's needs and wants in a conflict.

Finally, when you underuse compromise, you might be relying too heavily on the Competing Approach, which can severely damage relationships with others (we'll talk more about this in chapter 5). When you compete too much, you're often pushing for personal gain, control, or pleasure rather than building a connection with the people you care about most. If you try to compete rather than compromise with me too often, I may learn to go around your back to meet my needs. I may also refuse to engage in conflict with you at all if I know that you won't consider my offers, opinions, and feelings.

What are the ideal conditions for the Compromising Approach?

Compromising often works best when you have to make quick, fair decisions. Rather than deliberate or hesitate, you must meet challenges with brief, sharply focused negotiations.

Several years ago, I visited with a colleague and client named John who was frustrated about his constant parenting battles with Pat, his ex-wife. John had some pretty immediate concerns about his son's academic abilities and wanted to act on those impressions before things got out of hand.

"I know that we both love Scott," John began, "but we completely disagree about what he needs. He's still young enough at 10 years old to listen to us, but he's got to be confused because we're each telling him different things. Personally, I think he's got some real learning disabilities, but Pat refuses to see it. She thinks I'm reading something into the situation that's not there."

As John relayed his concerns about Pat's dismissal of Scott's possible learning disabilities and her harsher, more authoritarian parenting style, we began discussing possible steps forward. I was curious to see if they'd had any previous successes with conflict resolution outside of the official court system, which John considered to be too costly and time-consuming for this issue. He wanted to act more quickly than the courts would allow.

"John, it's been a few years since you've been separated now. What's worked so far?" I asked gently.

"We've been to this decision-maker who's kind of like a mini-judge."

"How's that gone? Do you agree with his judgements?"

John recounted several visits with the decision-maker who provided judgments about John's and Pat's joint-parenting decisions. John didn't say that he was skeptical about the judgments, so I questioned him a bit further.

"So, are you interested in using the decision-maker again? And, if so, would Pat ever accept the option of getting Scott tested for possible learning disabilities, if the decision-maker suggested it?"

"She really liked the decision-maker, so I think that's an actual possibility. Of course, we'd have to see if he's available sometime soon, but that just might work." John finally looked a little more upbeat.

While John would have preferred to get his son tested immediately without Pat's permission, he knew that would ultimately create more tension with his ex-wife that could spill over and hurt their son. Consulting a more neutral decision-maker that he knew Pat accepted would be better than trying to go around her back. He told me he wished they could just talk things through and come to an agreement, but if that wasn't an option, this would have to be the next best thing for their son, whom they both loved.

Beyond more intense child custody battles, every day we encounter situations that demand some give and take. Let's consider some ideal situations for using this approach to constructively resolve a variety of conflicts.

1. *You need a quick resolution.*

In our busy lives, we must quickly and decisively make many decisions that affect other people. I'm sure the Coronavirus pandemic created new situations for you that demanded timely decisions to balance work and family responsibilities. In the spring of 2020, the university where I work reopened and my children returned to school only two days a week at reduced hours. I had one week to figure out how to be present both at work and at home when needed. While I would have preferred being on campus every day during office hours, I hired a student to cover for me when my children's schools got out so I could take care of them. As a compromise, I worked two days a week from home and two days a week on campus to balance out my home and work responsibilities—this represents a good, quick compromise to balance personal responsibilities and interests.

2. *Power is relatively balanced between the two parties.*

Many years ago, I lived in a lovely little house in Arlington, Virginia, with four roommates. As the last roommate to arrive, I acquired the basement bedroom located just below the living room where roommates and friends regularly congregated late at night. Given that I had a job and a commute each morning, I was concerned about getting a good night's sleep. After many difficult nights when I couldn't fall asleep because of the footsteps and voices I could hear from the room above me, I called a roommate meeting to talk about the issue.

I had expected that my roommates would easily accept my idea of having a "sound" curfew around 10 p.m. Instead, one of my roommates asked if I could start wearing earplugs. At first, I was offended that she suggested earplugs rather than assuming that the other roommates, including herself, needed to be quieter, but I decided to compromise in the interest of harmony. I started wearing ear plugs the next day, and that actually fixed the problem.

3. *The goals of both parties have equal importance, merit, and truly appear incompatible.*

My husband and I stand divided about our sons playing tackle football. Despite my love of sports, I worry about my sons playing football because of the risk of injury, especially concussions. My husband loves the sport and was not encouraged to play when he was younger, so he feels he missed out on an opportunity to thrive athletically. Knowing my husband's passion for the game and his desire to let our sons choose for themselves, I know that I cannot prohibit my sons from playing.

Our second son made the football team, and sometimes I struggle to let him make his own decisions about playing. I regularly share my fears and worries and try to offer other athletic enticements to my son, like volleyball or ultimate frisbee. Part of our compromise in letting our sons play involves me regularly reminding our children about the dangers of the sport and urging them to dabble in other sports where they might find more success and less risk.

Over time, my husband and I have converged on a greater compromise position that emphasizes each child's ability to choose what he or she would like to play as a sport. As my children get older and become more aware of the hazards of each sport, I'm becoming more comfortable with that compromise. In this case, we compromised because we each have strong feelings about our positions, which we will not easily change.

4. *The parties opposing us resist collaboration, competing or collaboration modes are not working, and you need a secondary or back-up approach. We use compromise to avoid a stalemate.*

My husband and I compromise about our sons playing tackle football because we have not been able to arrive at a collaborative approach (which I'll discuss in chapter 6) and we do not want to compete with each other. In this case, compromise is an interim conflict resolution approach that allows us to preserve our relationship and avoid a stalemate (making no decision at all).

5. *Complete achievement of our goals is not important.*

Nearly every night, my 10-year-old daughter and I negotiate about how much of her current book-in-progress we will read together. Usually, my daughter can expect that I'll read at least one chapter with her, but she often pushes for more. Sometimes, she waits until she finishes brushing her teeth or snuggles right next to me to ask, "Just one more page, please, Mama?"

Depending on how tired I am I may give in to her wishes, but on other nights I say firmly, "I'm just too tired tonight." Either way, we enjoy our time together, sometimes reading many pages, and on other nights only reading a few. We don't intend to read the whole book in one sitting, so we're each comfortable without complete achievement of our different goals. My goal is to get her to sleep, and hers is to read as much as possible!

6. *There are multiple potential solutions that appeal to the parties in the conflict.*

When I began my current job, our staff gathered to discuss how to balance out the part-time schedules of our center's four staff members to create regular office hours for our clients. As we brainstormed together, we developed several viable options that would fit our staff members' schedules and our clients' needs. In the end, we selected a part-time option that gave me Fridays off, which I appreciated but hadn't imagined possible at the beginning of the brainstorming. This compromise process involved brainstorming but didn't include the more in-depth conversation and sharing that resembles true collaboration.

7. *There will be no hard feelings between people for settling for less than expected.*

Recently I went used car shopping for my teenagers, which I never really enjoy because I have to make a fairly significant purchase on something good enough to live with but not so good that it will cost me more than I want to pay. I'm just not a "let's get a 'C' in the class" kind of girl, but used car shopping for a teenage driver feels like that kind of game—a series of compromises involving bartering with a salesperson about a so-so car.

I had already negotiated with my husband about getting our teenagers a car, so I was a little worn out at the dealership. But I came prepared with an upper price limit in mind. As we sat down at the desk to hammer out the details of the car sale, small red flags popped up. I couldn't help but smile when I saw the $99 car prep fee for washing the car before I got to drive it home. *Seriously?* $99 for something that usually costs $5? Because the car price itself fit within my parameters, I chose to pay a couple hundred extra dollars in order to quickly complete the deal and go home. I had no hard feelings about letting the dealership take small advantage of me, even though it came up unexpectedly at the end of the deal making. The salesman had planned it that way, right?!

You might not have made the same decision as I did that day, but I consciously chose to stay out of conflict by settling for something less than expected because I could accept the outcome before me.

We each have to decide how we will spend our time and money in negotiating with others for the things we desire. This is the essence of the Compromising Approach.

As always, you should seek balance among the Five Conflict Approaches to avoid unnecessary contention and build stable, loving relationships with others based on trust and true sharing. Adding compromise to your conflict resolution tool belt, or merely readjusting when and how you use it, can improve how we feel about ourselves and how others feel about us.

Questions for Reflection

---

1. When am I most likely to compromise?

2. How do I feel about the compromises I make?

3. Would I change the things I compromise about?

4. Would I change the people with whom I compromise?

5. What situations in my life seem most appropriate for compromise?

THE COMPROMISING APPROACH:

THINGS TO REMEMBER

In conflict resolution based on compromising, each party settles for *partial* satisfaction of their interests by giving up something that they want in order to resolve the conflict.

When and why you might use the Compromising Approach:

- The Compromising Approach may help settle a conflict quickly in a socially acceptable way.
- You might get anxious when you have to deal with conflict. In your anxiety, you may want the conflict to be over as soon as possible, so you offer to compromise, even if it does not benefit you—and often doesn't actually benefit the other person, either.
- You may choose to compromise because you're pressed for time and need to make a quick decision while still providing an air of fairness and respect for the relationship.
- Compromise may also help you avoid a tricky or overly tense situation.
- Compromise may also help demonstrate your self-confidence while still respecting someone else's goals and interests.

Benefits:

- Compromise is generally considered fast and efficient.
- This approach is easily understood and applied by others in Western culture.
- With compromise, the conflict is removed and relationships are usually maintained.
- Compromise is a culturally acceptable way of dealing with conflict.

Drawbacks:

- Each party in a conflict must give up something to resolve the conflict (so in that sense it's a lose-lose situation).
- Compromise may not provide you with what you desire, and when you get only part of what you want, the conflict may perpetuate.
- Compromise decisions may require close monitoring and control to ensure that people follow through with what they have agreed to.
- This approach does not usually contribute to building trust in the long run.
- Compromise may reflect an inability to connect on a deeper level over difficult issues.
- When you compromise too much and too quickly in important relationships, you may miss opportunities to collaborate and dig deeper into your and the other party's needs, desires, and expectations.
- If you compromise without thoughtful reflection, you may be disregarding some of your important

values and long-term objectives, leaving you in a worse position than when you started.

Overusing the Compromising Approach:

- If you compromise too often and too quickly, you may feel resentment or even "buyer's remorse," believing you have paid too high a price for the compromise resolution.
- When you overuse compromise to bypass important issues, you may get to an important point in your life when you realize that you long for real understanding and collaboration.
- Your acceptance or extension of compromise decisions may represent your inability or discomfort in showing who you really are and may exacerbate your sense of loneliness or alienation from others.

Underusing the Compromising Approach:

- If you're experiencing or even just perceiving too little social power and hardly any compromise in your life, you may be using avoiding and accommodating too often.
- In your desire to demonstrate empathy and excellent listening, you may be spending too much time and energy trying to collaborate about conflict situations that would benefit from less investment and a quicker turnaround time.
- If you underuse compromise, you might be relying too heavily on the Competing Approach, which can severely damage relationships with others.

Ideal Conditions for the Compromising Approach:

1. You need quick resolution of issues.
2. Power is relatively balanced between the two parties.
3. The goals of both parties have equal importance, merit, and truly appear incompatible.
4. The parties opposing you resist collaboration, competing or collaboration modes are not working, and you need a back-up approach to avoid a stalemate.
5. Complete achievement of your goals is not important.
6. There are multiple potential solutions that appeal to the parties in the conflict.
7. There will be no hard feelings between people for settling for less than expected.

Chapter 5

Conflict Approach #4: Competing

As part of my conflict resolution training in grad school, I took a fascinating class devoted to practicing the principles of *persuasion*. Rather than writing research papers, my professor, Dr. Silva, required that we use persuasion in real-life situations to get people to do things for us—quite a test for someone like me who usually avoids and accommodates!

As I pulled up one of the first assignments online, I sighed. I was supposed to approach a service provider about a poorly rendered service and seek compensation. This reminded me of how my great-grandmother Dougan used to stand up and clap her hands to get a waiter's attention—it always made me cringe! She was a rich old lady who seemed comfortable bossing people around, but I was pretty sure I hadn't inherited that gene. I hated the thought of taking a competitive or aggressive stance in public.

I'd once asked a waiter for a new salad when I found a fly buzzing around in my lettuce, but I had never asked a store owner to pony up and apologize for something. To get an "A" in this class, I had to *do something* to find out if the principles we were studying worked. I had to take a Competing Approach to win.

I thought about the haphazard skin cancer treatment I'd recently received at my dermatology clinic. I had already gotten five or six blue light treatments for my squamous and basal cell carcinoma, and I knew that my last treatment had been sloppy. But how was I going to get up the nerve to confront my doctor? Why should I create unnecessary friction in our otherwise good relationship?

With the class deadline looming, I worked up my courage and called the dermatologist. I asked the office staff to redo my skin treatment. To my surprise, the admin quickly responded to my request and told me that the doctor would call me back soon. I was still questioning myself as I waited for his call. *Do I actually want to have this conversation?* But I did it.

"Dr. Stanley, I could just tell that the treatment was not spread evenly on my face and didn't have the same effect as usual. I'd like to have the treatment done again."

After hearing my concerns, Dr. Stanley agreed and suggested that I contact the office staff again to schedule another treatment free-of-charge. I couldn't believe it was that easy. I'd won.

Like an actress playing a role, for each assignment I would follow the script of persuasion principles that helped me *compete* rather than shrink from a problem. And I always wound up with exactly what I'd asked for. The first few times the discussions felt crazy, but then I realized they were just different from what I'd been brought up to do when faced with an interpersonal dilemma. I usually had little to lose when I would try this approach, which freed me from some of the fear I would otherwise feel by being so bold.

As an adult, I've learned to be more competitive and persuasive in social situations when I would normally back down. Part of the challenge for me is in the word "competition." If you're like me, images of NFL players bulldozing each other down or a boxer throwing the knock-out punch in a Vegas ring may swirl in your mind when you think of "competing." We're surrounded by images of athletes, businesspeople, government leaders, and other public figures using their power to *coerce* others to gain a victory over someone else. Our culture ties all kinds of dirty, sarcastic, and aggressive thoughts, feelings, and behaviors to the idea of competition. We justify a lot of bad behavior by saying, "That's just how it is," as if human nature dictates the survival of those who will stoop lowest and fight dirtiest. I'm still uncomfortable with that interpretation of competition.

You don't have to go far to see evidence of how acceptable negative versions of competition have become. During a youth sports match, I heard parents cheer their children on with refrains like: "Get angry!" "Be aggressive!" Over and over, parents encouraged their children to harness their anger to overpower the other children facing them across the field. I couldn't help but think of the crowds in ancient Rome who witnessed the gladiators' battles in arenas full of angry people living vicariously through a brutal competition. We have become so comfortable putting competition on display in sports, our market economy, and even in our education system, that we often justify the worst outcomes as the natural consequences of a fair competition.

So you may wonder why I even suggest the Competing Approach as a truly legitimate and essential tool in our conflict resolution skill set. It's because competing is much more than being angry or using aggression to overpower another person or group. Competition is about *not yielding your position or desires to another* but seeking to fulfill your own goals when faced with opposition from a person or group.

Believe me, competitive conflict resolution can be achieved without hostility or aggression. I see it work all the time.

Nonviolence and love are possible *within* a Competing Approach. The civil rights protestors of the 1960s understood that sitting firmly in a forbidden seat or getting back up every time someone brutally beats you down on a bridge is competitive in nature. But those actions need not be angry or violent in feeling or presentation. We see so many moments in history when one person's firm, unyielding, competing stance benefitted entire groups of people who were being oppressed.

What is the Competing Approach?

I barely noticed the crowd eating breakfast around me in a suburban Village Inn a few years ago as I began a job interview. Despite my initial hesitation about the interview, I grew more confident with each question the gorgeous blonde sales manager, Cat, asked me. In the downturn of 2002, I really needed a good job like this one, especially with my new husband starting graduate school. I couldn't afford to be super picky about industry or title, and I didn't want to squander my friend's referral that had given me an "in" with Cat. I needed to market myself the best that I could, despite my lack of direct sales experience.

Glancing down at my resume, Cat asked: "It appears that you have no direct pharmaceutical sales training. Can you help me understand what experience you bring to the position?"

I had been expecting that question and was ready. I looked straight into Cat's eyes and rattled off a series of credentials that served as quasi-sales experience. Any hesitation left me, because I could tell that she was buying my pitch and that I was successfully selling myself right then and there. She knew it, and I knew it.

I didn't leave that breakfast with an offer in hand, but I knew I had convinced her I could fill her position. Rather than apologizing for the gaps in my resume, I filled them with relevant information. I *competed* for her belief in my talents and skills, and she bought it.

Like I did in winning that sales job, when competing in conflict, you can actively seek to reach your own personal goals, especially when it appears that others might not cooperate. With a Competing Approach, you clearly demonstrate your power and/or abilities to achieve personal goals.

You might be tempted to set a tone of domination or authority to establish power in relationships where there have been abuses and/or imbalances. At times, you may even try to instill fear in the other party to preserve stability and harmony in current and future social situations. Like stopping a toddler from wandering into the middle of the road, sometimes quick, decisive action is needed to preserve life and ensure peace.

Constructive competitive thoughts and actions ideally flow from a compassionate and kind heart that avoids conflict escalation and hostility, both of which derail conflict resolution processes.

When and why do people use the Competing Approach?

Sometimes, only after unsuccessful efforts to avoid, accommodate, or compromise, do we attempt to compete with others for what we need or want. Even outside the sports arena, there are times when a stronger, more direct use of power makes sense to achieve our desired results. When we compete, we don't necessarily use force or violence, but we stand for what we believe in without bending to others' wishes. In 2020, for example, we witnessed widespread competitive efforts to remove Confederate symbols from American public life across the United States.

Long after the Civil War, officials in many southern cities and states erected prominent Confederate statues in important public places such as capitol buildings, main streets, and parks to intimidate Black citizens and symbolize the continuing legacy of the Confederacy and slavery. With nearly 2,000 Confederate symbols throughout public lands in the South, most people couldn't avoid daily reminders of racial injustice. Many attempts were made to remove these monuments over the years, usually without success.

With the brutal death of George Floyd at the hands of Minneapolis police in May 2020, protests erupted throughout the United States and worldwide over longstanding racial injustice. Rather than stand by, thousands of citizens gathered to remove symbols of the Confederacy by physical force and through the force of law via the courts, legislatures, and city councils.

Following the brisk toppling of several statues by protestors in Richmond, Virginia, the former Confederate capital, elected officials joined forces with the citizens' movement and called for the removal of all Confederate symbols from Virginia's public spaces. Stymied by opponents who tried to block local officials' efforts to remove these statues, the question went to the Virginia Supreme Court. In Spring 2021, the Court ruled that cities had the right to remove these statues, which represented the worst of Southern culture, past and present.

Noting what I would call a Competing Approach to removing the statues, Virginia Attorney General Mark R. Herring announced:

"I have worked hard to help remove poisonous Confederate propaganda from our publicly owned spaces, because I believe it glorifies a false history and sends a dangerous and divisive message about who and what we value."[14]

Softer approaches tried over previous decades in many states had not worked. Yet, spurred on by the tragedies of 2020, protestors and lawmakers gained courage and used the power of numbers, increased visibility, and critical public sentiment to build momentum and push for needed change. The moment was ripe for action, and people seized the opportunity.

As demonstrated by recent changes in the South and elsewhere, competition is a difficult strategy to manage well, but it is an important tool for conflict resolution in many social situations.

Many of us grow up participating in highly competitive activities, including sports, music, and academics. Given the anxiety levels many people feel today, competition can be highly destructive to our self-confidence. It can affect our desire to belong and matter in the world. A competing conflict resolution approach brings balance and justice to our designs for mercy, compassion, and peace. Common reasons for using the Competing Approach in conflict include:

- We're willing to fight for what we want without concern for how it will affect our relationships.

- We're pressed for time.

- We're in danger and need to make decisions quickly.

- We're used to getting what we want and demanding that our needs and wants are fulfilled.

- People defer to us because of inherent power structures, such as title, wealth, or prestige.

- We stand behind principles that are not being acknowledged or treated properly.

- We represent less powerful people and ideas that need strong representation.

Through my own personal experiences, I've learned how essential competing in conflict can be, not just to win, but also to create harmony and balance in my relationships.

Growing up, I pursued a variety of interests. I participated in competitive club soccer, gymnastics, and student government. I loved to ski black diamond runs at Lake Tahoe and audition for school plays. Whether in sports, theatre, academics, or student government, I faced many competitors and always tried to do my best. I didn't see any problem with competing in areas of life expressly set up with competition in mind, but I never liked competition among friends. When I encountered social differences, I usually tried to make room for others and avoid creating enemies. All my life, I've disliked exclusion and sought to help others feel comfortable and valued, which must be one reason I got into the world of mediation.

With kindness as my main strategy, I focused on conflict prevention and avoidance more than conflict resolution in its own right. For me, kindness meant relying on self-sacrifice and patience as primary ways of avoiding conflict in the first place. I believed people didn't have to compete with those they loved because those they loved would naturally listen and try to accommodate them.

As an independent and ambitious person, I forged my own path and worked to create the life I wanted. My conflict prevention strategy worked pretty well when I was single, although I sometimes failed to secure deeper relationships because I avoided dealing with more confrontational people who might have pushed me beyond my comfortable emotional boundaries.

I was idealistic about marriage despite several divorces in my family. I imagined that my spouse and I would be so compatible that we wouldn't need to negotiate regularly. Surely, we would be so alike that we would work out minor disagreements easily and see most issues from the same perspective. In fact, I looked for partners who seemed most similar to me in terms of temperament, hobbies, talents, and life ambitions. No opposites attract for me! I believed conflict led to divorce, and I wanted to avoid that at all costs.

How wrong I was to think I could avoid all conflict! I share many important values with my husband, but I fell in love with a competitive person who often pushes back on my ideas. I never expected that I would marry someone who dealt with conflict so differently.

Over many years with Ken, I've learned that marriage is a relationship that demands great flexibility and conflict fluency.

By flexing my competitive conflict resolution muscles in the right situations, I've begun to find marital connections and personal growth that I don't think would have been possible otherwise. Without daily, personal experiences expanding my well-worn Avoiding and Accommodating Approaches, I would have missed out on becoming a more well-rounded and confident person. I've struggled with loneliness and self-doubt, as we all do, but with studied effort and trial and error, I've tried new approaches to conflict and grown immensely. I've learned to show up with a full range strategies and attitudes to resolve differences.

If you are not used to using the Competitive Approach, you can definitely learn. You will need to practice, and you will make mistakes along the way. But with courage and persistence, you will begin to see positive changes in yourself and your relationships.

And if you *are* inclined to compete with others in conflict, you can learn to expand your tool kit of approaches and experience refreshingly different outcomes, especially with those you love. Rather than seeking domination in most or all social situations, you will learn to share power more easily with others, increasing feelings of connection. Instead of fearing your disapproval or use of force, those you care about will be drawn to you in a partnership where they can share ideas easily and find mutually satisfying solutions to the problems you face together.

What are the benefits?

I was nervous to meet with Dean Thomas about my application to law school. As a mother of five in my late forties, I wondered if I had it in me to get through the courses and exams. Would she see right through my smile and know how anxious I was about my recent lame GRE math score?

Dean Thomas motioned for me to sit down while she seated herself behind a large and formal desk. I sat in the stiff brown chair a few feet away and looked out at the snow-covered mountains through the massive window.

After a moment's pause, I handed her my resume and began chatting about my experiences. "So, I've been working in the law school for a year now and think I could add a lot to the community." I chronicled my initiative, experience, and will to succeed.

I just had to help her understand how much she would benefit from admitting me. I had already written a statement of purpose. If accepted, I promised I would take the LSAT to show her that I really could jump through all the hoops.

As if right on cue, a few weeks later, Dean Thomas called, "Emily, we'd like to accept you, but we need you to take the LSAT."

"Okay. Thank you! I'll sign up and start the class tomorrow," I said with butterflies of excitement fluttering in my stomach. I quickly enrolled in a prep class that started the next day. Then I threw out my plans for a peaceful Saturday with the kids at home and drove into campus for a 3 ½ hour class that included a full practice LSAT.

I had never looked at the LSAT, so this was an example of me jumping in the deep end without a life jacket. After the instructor said, "You may begin," I raced to read through difficult texts and logic questions at breakneck speed. I was shocked to see that the test wasn't impossible, but it required such quick thinking that I knew I needed serious preparation.

"I could do this test, if I really studied for it. There's nothing beyond me here," I reassured myself as I started the next section. But something shifted in my thinking as I sat at that hard wooden desk surrounded by younger, equally stressed-out classmates.

I continued a surprising inner dialogue, "I could study for the LSAT during the next few months, but I don't want to. I don't want to give up all my Saturdays and weeknights for studying. Wow! I know what I want now. I don't want this, and that's okay."

After this powerful epiphany, I sat quietly pretending to take the rest of the test, but my mind relaxed and my spirit finally settled in on the truth: "I don't want to go to law school."

After months of explanations to friends and family defending why I *wanted* to go to law school, I had arrived at my own truth.

Competing to get into law school provided the necessary stress to reveal to me what I really desired. The competitive situation forced my hand. I gained critical self-knowledge that I don't think I could have found any other way.

Sometimes you don't just compete with others; you compete with yourself. Do you have the tools to push back against fear, doubt, and misunderstanding, whether it comes from the inside or the outside? Competing is all about advocating for your own interests in any situation. You don't have to be mean or nasty about standing up for what you want or need, but you will need some stamina when you meet opposition.

Again, please remember that competing in conflict doesn't always involve hostility, anger, and aggression. The everyday person who lives a very ordinary life may benefit immensely from strategically using the Competing Approach without intense aggression or hostility. Some benefits include:

- We might "win" the entire conflict and get everything we wanted from the beginning.

- We might get what we want more quickly if we don't care about other people's feelings.

- When we consistently assert our position, we may also establish our dominance in a social setting.

- We can set a precedent of power and authority, or even rebalance power after we've lost it, which will influence future conflict outcomes.

- We can demonstrate our commitment to a certain position or an ideal. Others may take our position more seriously if they see that we're not willing to back down when it becomes inconvenient or even dangerous.

Competitive conflict approaches help balance otherwise imbalanced power structures, but there are risks associated with using the Competing Approach, especially in times of societal polarization like we're experiencing now. To buffer our tendency to either overuse or underuse the competing conflict approach, we should also consider the very real drawbacks of using the competing conflict approach on a regular basis.

What are the drawbacks?

Driving her minivan along the main drag in suburbia, Olivia didn't think much about her upcoming turn onto the freeway to pick up her kids from preschool. She had driven this road so many times she could almost do it on auto-pilot.

As she turned right onto the ramp, she noticed an electric blue BMW turning onto the same ramp from the opposite direction. The driver seemed to be edging toward the very same lane she was about to enter.

Rather than slow down, Olivia pressed the gas to cut ahead. She looked into her rearview mirror to see him flash her an angry look as he then sped to her side in the adjacent freeway lane.

She tried to speed up to avoid the awkward situation, but he kept pace with her. "What should I do?" she asked out loud, as she started to panic. "Why is he still following me?"

When she signaled to exit the freeway, he followed close behind her, exiting too. Her heart pounded as he trailed her into the smaller streets near her child's preschool.

Finally, she turned into the small lane with the preschool just ahead of her, and the other driver decided against following her any farther. As she parked her car in the preschool parking lot, her hands were folded tightly over her chest, and she was breathing deeply to calm down.

Olivia had not meant to openly compete with this driver, but he had taken her sudden speed as confrontational. His show of force and desire to intimidate Olivia created intense feelings of fear and tension for her. By competitively reacting to her simple choice to accelerate onto the freeway ramp ahead of him, he turned an ordinary situation into a high stakes confrontation that could have led to a more severe ending.

This small road rage incident demonstrates some natural drawbacks of the Competing Approach. This approach to conflict involves scenarios of dominance and submission with winners and losers. In competitive situations, usually one party is not happy about the outcomes.

- When we use the competitive approach too frequently, we may be perceived by less powerful parties as power-hungry, selfish, and uncooperative.

- The parties who "lose" may create back channels that help them get what they want, regardless of our use of power or disapproval. Think of people who sell goods on the black market or rebellious teenagers who slip out through bedroom windows after curfew.

- If we use a competitive approach too regularly in our most important, intimate relationships, this may result in resentment and defiance. When we use force to realize our personal goals, we may permanently damage a relationship.

- Responding to the competitive approach may be draining and stressful if we prefer a less aggressive way of resolving conflict.

- If we're overly aggressive or nasty when we use the Competing Approach, we will probably escalate conflict intensity and frequency with others and even within ourselves.

In light of these many drawbacks, we can all benefit from understanding what happens to us and others when we either overuse or underuse this approach.

What happens when you overuse the Competing Approach?

After a busy day meeting with clients, Dr. Chang finally found himself resting alone in his medical office. Unlike the hospital where he went from procedure to procedure, in his private office, he actually had a little downtime between patients.

Dr. Chang tensed a little when his medical assistant, Trish, knocked on the door and poked her head in. "Dr. Chang, there's a sales rep here to see you. What do you want me to tell him?"

Dr. Chang looked down, sighed, and asked, "Who is it? Anyone I know?"

"It's Tom, the one who sells the statins."

"Oh, yeah, Tom—is he the guy who keeps visiting every week?"

Trish looked sympathetic and said, "Yes, he brought us bagels and coffee on Tuesday and has followed up with a couple of messages since then. Seems like he's really eager to talk to you about their new drug."

Wearily, Dr. Chang tried to refresh his memory of Tom. "Is that the tall young guy that talked for half an hour when I let him in a couple months ago?"

"Yes. He's a nice guy, just pretty gung-ho about making his sales."

"I just don't have time to listen to a sales spiel right now. Please let him know that I'm too busy today."

Trish nodded, "Do you want me to give him a time to come back?"

"Yeah, how about you make me an appointment with him next month when I have a fifteen-minute slot so we can keep it short."

When we compete for people's attention or treat others as objects to be acted upon, we risk ruining real chances to connect. Some people do everything they can to avoid contact with us if they know that they are being used for selfish purposes.

When you overuse the Competing Approach— especially in your more important social relationships—you risk weakening or destroying valuable social relationships. You risk losing the trust of people who begin to question your motives. Those we oppose in conflict will probably seek to develop back channels to get what they want without having to confront us. For example, if I constantly refuse to let my children play video games, they may decide to find a way to play that is outside of my control, like at a friend's house.

Remember all the illegal activity that cropped up during the Prohibition era in the United States? While many citizens supported the ban on alcohol, the legal action of banning it through a constitutional amendment created the impetus for many citizens to go "underground." This did not necessarily create a healthier outcome for individuals and the population at large. Or consider the thriving black market of the former Soviet Union. When regular stores wouldn't carry what people in Soviet Russia wanted, sellers of those goods went underground, along with many other kinds of forbidden activities, including protests against the government. When there's a will or a desire, people always find a way.

How we resolve conflict may often be just as important as the conflict itself. We need to be careful when we use competitive tactics in especially tricky social dilemmas because of unintended consequences, including people creating more dangerous situations by going underground.

I'm not saying that we should *not* compete with others in a variety of conflict situations, but I *am* saying that if we use too much coercion, we might fail to achieve our goals. I think of the "rude American" who tries to speak English wherever she goes, no matter the nation or country she is visiting. On the flip side, a savvy traveler tries to adapt to new cultures, languages, and customs. Like this traveler, we should expect diversity and prepare to meet challenging differences with a variety of approaches to conflict, drawing from a large tool bag of skills and perspectives. You have more options than just dominating or submitting in any given conflict situation.

What happens when you underuse the Competing Approach?

Many years ago as a missionary in southern Japan, I had the harrowing experience of being isolated and ostracized by fellow missionaries who I considered to be my teammates. My difficulties really began when I became a trainer to a Japanese companion, Sister Suzuki, who could culturally relate to the many young women we were already teaching when she arrived.

A couple of the male missionaries in my group took the initiative to reach out to work with Sister Suzuki, but they did so in a way that alienated and estranged me. Rather than confer with me as Sister Suzuki's trainer, Elder Johnson called our apartment and asked to speak with Sister Suzuki on her own. Elder Johnson was in a position of authority over me, so everything he did carried a lot of weight.

He eventually asked to see Sister Suzuki in his office while I was left to sit outside in the church hallway by myself feeling unneeded, disrespected, and superfluous.

One afternoon in our English class, I was teaching a bright young teenage girl a lesson about Jesus, when Elder Johnson opened the church classroom door, pulled up a chair, and began teaching the lesson in my place. As a further blow to my confidence, he temporarily transferred me to another city to "pop [my] pride bubble," as he put it.

In the southern city of Kumamoto for a conference, I remember sitting by myself on a cold metal chair in deep despair. When I looked up, I noticed a man I remembered as Elder Williams walking up to me with a concerned look on his face.

"Are you okay?" he asked.

I knew he had a reputation for being sincere and kind, so I answered honestly, "No, I'm not," and then started crying.

He ushered me toward an empty classroom where we sat for almost 40 minutes as I poured out my heartache. For more than two months, I had tried to shoulder my loneliness without advocating or competing for my needs to be met. In retrospect, I think I could have advocated for myself and created a healthier situation, but I didn't understand that at the time.

With careful attention, Elder Williams listened to me as I revealed the hurt of the past several months. Soon after our conversation, he facilitated my transfer to another city. Advocating for myself eventually brought relief and new opportunities.

When you don't stand up for your needs or rights, people can and will walk all over you. In Japan, I first felt inferior, then infuriated and alienated. I've gradually learned that it's worth standing up for myself in order to be happy and at peace.

When we underuse the Competing Approach, we may become frustrated with or completely avoid those who constantly compete with us. An obvious consequence of underusing the Competing Approach with competitive people is that you will constantly "lose" in conflict. Potential losses for the non-competitor include never getting to voice an opinion, never pushing back on ideas they disagree with, never gaining stakes in the game plans, and missing out on leadership opportunities.

When you keep losing in competitive conflict resolution, you also lose a sense of autonomy and choice. This may lead you to experience chronic stress and even deep bouts of hopelessness and despair. Without being able to deeply influence conflict outcomes you care about, you lose motivation to keep going in the same direction, or you just give up. For example, when you encounter a boss who constantly pushes back on all your ideas, you'll probably store up resentment that will eventually lead you to quit.

Unfortunately, some of us are not taught how to compete constructively, so we just avoid the approach entirely. This might especially be true if we hated how others, such as an abusive parent or school bully, competed with us in the past. Rather than become the abuser or the bully ourselves, we just avoid the Competing Approach entirely because we don't want to hurt, shame, or dominate others.

We need to learn how to compete for the *right reasons* and with a controlled and compassionate attitude to avoid contention.

I can advocate for my child without blowing up and trying to tear down a teacher or coach who I believe has treated my child unfairly. And as a parent competing with my child, I will be much more successful in disciplining and teaching if I can control my temper and remain consistent with family rules and norms.

Of course, we're all subject to moments when we lose control, but we can usually come out with some solid gains if we keep specific goals and attitudes in mind while competing.

What are the ideal conditions for using the Competing Approach?

In 1840, my tiny 4'11" Quaker great-grandmother, Lucretia Mott, attended the World Anti-Slavery Convention in London as one of the official U.S. delegates. However, she was restricted from participating in formal convention activities because she was a woman. White male delegates at the convention actually pointed to their Bibles as their authority, telling her that it was the will of God that only men participate.

While barred from officially participating in the convention, Lucretia did not back down quietly. Instead, after the convention closed, she and prominent fellow abolitionist, William Lloyd Garrison, spoke to a crowd of more than 500 people at the Crown & Anchor Meeting Hall. She eloquently and unabashedly refuted the men's claims about the rightness of women's subjugation to their husbands, saying that it was "law and public opinion" that kept women out of the meeting, not the Bible's teachings. Lucretia's progressive calls for equality outside of the convention halls earned her the nickname, "Lioness of London."

For the next forty years, Lucretia continued to advocate for equal rights for women and people of color and took competitive action to back up her lively speeches. To put financial pressure on the Southern slave-based economy, the Mott family refused to use products produced by enslaved people's labor, including sugar and cotton, and encouraged others to boycott them. Lucretia even convinced her husband, James, to switch his textile company's focus to woolen cloth to avoid any entanglement with Southern cotton. In word and deed, the Motts used a Competing Approach to fight dominant beliefs about women and Blacks in their day, working to shift their society toward greater justice.[15]

Few things expose your true values more than when someone tells you that you can't do something important, as those delegates told my great-grandmother. While I don't advocate for competing at every turn with those who disagree with you, there are certainly critical moments to advocate for the values you hold dear. If you don't, who will? And, if you don't compete now, will you eventually lose more than you have already lost?

In addition to helping us advocate for important causes, competing serves us in a variety of ways.

1. *You need to make decisions quickly.*

A parent grabs a wandering child to keep him from walking into a busy street, or a company director defends a joint management decision made after considerable deliberation. In both cases, people fix their focus on goals that need to be accomplished in a quick and immediate way, despite potential opposition. You're going to experience situations in which the time to consult, ponder, and debate just isn't there, and you must act decisively.

2. *Your options in conflict are restricted and personal opinions may be difficult to change.*

Some conflict situations don't allow for a wide variety of options to resolve the issues of all parties. You may encounter conflict situations between people with extremely strong opinions who are unwilling to change or brainstorm with you. In such cases, when you encounter restricted options for resolution and intractable personal positions around the conflict, you might benefit from applying a competitive conflict approach.

3. *You have nothing to lose by pushing for what you want.*

You'll sometimes encounter situations in which you have nothing to lose by asking for what you need or want. By competing, you may be even more likely to get the outcome that you want.

4. *The other parties in the conflict resist cooperating and will try to take advantage of you if you don't respond in a competitive way.*

In many social situations, you'll first try reaching out to others with a cooperative approach. If you're rebuffed or treated poorly, you might then choose to compete instead.

5. *You're not concerned about potential damage to the relationship.*

When you don't care about the relationship or the people you're in conflict with, it is usually much easier to compete. Whether you are a careless driver in the lane next to me or simply a name on a social media post, I will probably be more likely to compete with you to get what I want. I have less to lose in terms of a relationship because you are a stranger.

6. *The group may benefit from an unpopular decision that needs to be implemented.*

Some decisions made by government, church, or industry leaders are unpopular with the masses but reflect competitive decisions that will benefit society or the organization at large. Consider the painfully political and contentious decisions made by local, state, and national leaders to curb the spread of the Coronavirus by mandating the wearing of masks. Most people don't enjoy wearing masks, but government representatives make decisions for the public good that no one person can create in isolation.

Learning to compete well without escalating conflict unnecessarily is a highly desirable skill that we can acquire with diligent effort. Think of the competitive tactics of Mahatma Gandhi, Lucretia Mott, Martin Luther King, Jr., and other civil rights protestors of the past and present. These individuals consciously chose competitive tactics to change the world, and their nonviolence and peaceful manner created a platform for lasting influence and success.

We will never forget the activists in Selma, Birmingham, and throughout the South, who refused to strike back even when they were taunted and physically assaulted. Whether they were young people dining at the Woolworth's lunch counter or working men and women walking for hours to and from their jobs instead of using a segregated bus, these people combined their own individual competitive actions with the actions of others to help shift public opinion toward supporting justice for all.

In peacefully competing for principles and ideals, nonviolent heroes brought attention to their causes and influenced millions of people. Their manner of competing not only gave credibility to their causes but also *changed their opponents* in very real ways. Their style of peaceful and nonviolent competition curbed the tit-for-tat game that usually escalates conflict into an all-out war with an opposing force.

When we choose our tactics wisely, we can do better in influencing others through grounded, peaceful competitive conflict approaches at home, work, and throughout society.

Questions for Reflection

---

1. When do I compete with others to resolve conflict?

2. What has been my experience using competition to resolve conflict at work, at home, and in the community?

3. In what areas of my life could I benefit from using the Competitive Approach?

4. In what areas of my life could I benefit from using another approach?

5. What worries me about using the Competitive Approach in conflict?

6. How can I address my fears and try new ways of approaching conflicts in my life?

THE COMPETING APPROACH:

THINGS TO REMEMBER

In conflict resolution based on competing, you actively seek to reach your own personal goals, especially when others will not cooperate.

When and why you might use the Competing Approach:

- You're willing to fight for what you want without concern for how it will affect your relationships.
- You're used to getting what you want and demanding that your needs and wants are fulfilled.
- People defer to you because of inherent power structures, such as title, wealth, or prestige.
- You stand behind principles that are not being acknowledged or treated properly.
- You represent less powerful people and ideas that need representation.
- You're pressed for time.
- You're in danger and need to make decisions quickly.

Benefits:

- The most obvious benefit to using the Competing Approach is that you might "win" the entire conflict and (supposedly) get everything you want.
- You might get what you want more quickly if you don't care about other people's feelings.

- When you consistently assert your position, you may also establish your dominance in a social setting.
- When you compete, you can also set a precedent of power and authority, or even rebalance power after you've lost it, which will influence future conflict outcomes.
- Through competing, you are able to demonstrate your commitment to a certain position or an ideal. Others may take your position more seriously if they see that you're not willing to back down when it becomes inconvenient or even dangerous.

Drawbacks:

- Using the Competing Approach creates "winners" and "losers" in conflict. Usually, one party is not happy with the resolution.
- Those who frequently use the competitive approach may be perceived by less powerful parties as power-hungry, selfish, and uncooperative.
- The parties who "lose" in competitive conflict resolution may create back channels (like a black market) that help them get what they want regardless of your disapproval or use of power.
- If you use a competitive approach too regularly in your most important, intimate relationships, it may result in resentment and defiance. When you use force to realize your personal goals, you may permanently damage a relationship.
- Responding to the competitive approach may be draining and stressful for those who prefer a less aggressive way of resolving conflict.

- If you're overly aggressive or nasty when you use the Competing Approach, you will probably escalate conflict intensity and frequency between the parties or within yourself.

Overusing the Competing Approach:

- When you overuse the Competing Approach, especially in your more important social relationships, you risk weakening and even destroying those relationships.
- Those you compete with may learn to distrust your motives and expect game playing with winners and losers in even mundane conflicts.
- Those you oppose will likely seek to develop back channels to get what they want.

Underusing the Competing Approach:

- Many people who underuse the Competing Approach may become frustrated or avoid those who constantly compete with them.
- An obvious consequence of underusing the Competing Approach is that the non-competitor is constantly "losing" in conflict.
- Without a sense of autonomy and choice, many "losers" experience chronic stress and deep bouts of hopelessness or despair.
- Without the option to deeply influence conflict outcomes, you might lose motivation to keep going in the same direction or just give up on trying to influence outcomes.
- You may become explosive because you have tried to hold on in a losing pattern for too long.

Ideal Conditions for the Competing Approach:

1. You need to make decisions quickly.
2. Your options in conflict are restricted and personal opinions are difficult to change.
3. You have nothing to lose by pushing for what you want.
4. The other parties in the conflict resist cooperating and will try to take advantage of you if you don't respond in a competitive way.
5. You're not concerned about potential damage to the relationship.
6. The group may benefit from an unpopular decision that needs to be implemented.

Chapter 6

Conflict Approach #5: Collaborating

Many years ago, when our five children were small and extremely needy, my husband Ken proposed that we come up with a family motto. I resisted at first. It seemed like an idea he'd hatched based on a business school course, not based on the challenge of raising five little independent spirits who needed to become functional adults.

But with no HR manual to guide us (with all due respect to the dozens of helpful parenting books gifted from friends and family), I knew that we could use some sort of strategy to help us manage our family's seven robust personalities. So, I agreed to give the motto a try.

Predictably, Ken and I struggled to find consensus on a short, well-worded motto, and our disagreements occasionally got tense. I remember one especially uncomfortable dinner during what was supposed to be a couples' holiday retreat when Ken pulled out his notebook and announced, "Okay, so this is what we need to finish our vision…"

His pulling out the notebook during this romantic dinner annoyed me; it felt like a board meeting. I didn't want to have to negotiate with him over a touchy subject while I was actually *relaxing*. But rather than share my true feelings from the start, I half-heartedly joined in the conversation for a few minutes before telling him, "I just can't do this right now. I don't want to. Can we do it later?"

I'm sure Ken wondered what could possibly be a better time than this vacation, given our endless carpools, meal prep, homework help, laundry, and so on. Inevitably—and much to Ken's chagrin—I punted the conversation down the very busy road.

During the next year or two, whenever we got around to having a serious discussion about our motto, we couldn't seem to converge on a particular word or phrase to express the idea that we wanted our children to learn to choose good things in life. We were stuck.

We're both people of faith, but our religious sensibilities are quite different. I love old-fashioned—even archaic—terms, while Ken prefers modern language with emotional clarity. When we tried to translate our ideas into a single word, I chose "cleave," to emphasize holding on tenaciously to what's good. Ken chose "embrace," to reflect a whole-hearted acceptance of the good.

And the irony of our years-long standoff over a motto that was all about coming together as a family isn't lost on me.

I finally tried to capitulate after three years of debate. But I threw in the towel with what I knew was an annoying, self-sacrificing tone.

"*Fine,* we'll just use the word *you* like."

Ken could have taken offense and thrown back a nasty remark or taken a victory lap and gloated, but he didn't. He immediately answered with, "I can't allow you to give in because then it would be *my* motto and not *our* motto. It matters to me that we both really agree on it."

Looking back, I see his statement as a big turning point in our collaborative relationship. I felt boundless love and respect for Ken in that moment because he was able to set aside my lame attempt at accommodation. He knew how to look beyond the crisis of the moment and focus on the real goal—a motto that reflected both our goals, desires, and opinions.

A few weeks later, we arrived at a true consensus. I chose his word, *embrace,* but I did it independently, without coercion or bad feelings. Our family motto since then has been, "Come unto Christ. Embrace every good thing." We repeat it together during our family meetings every Sunday.

The important by-products of my husband's insistence that we collaborate on a joint task were more love, respect, and commitment in our marriage. In that moment, I understood that true collaboration is a rare gift that we give each other in our time-pressed, hyper-stressed lives.

How rarely do we experience another person's insistence that we collaborate in order to find the best solution for both of us?

When we slow down enough to work through the most important conflicts with our loved ones using a Collaborative Approach, we get to experience greater intimacy and respect for each other. Intimacy and respect are natural outcomes of taking the time and effort to truly understand the needs and wants of another person while still maintaining our own. In collaborating, we don't just self-sacrifice and move on as we do when accommodating. We exercise patience and put effort into developing mutually satisfying solutions.

What is the Collaborating Approach?

Jonah had not been talking with his brother, Greg, for several months and came to see me in my role as a mediator and coach. Jonah was upset because Greg seemed so accepting of their younger sister Sarah's gradual distancing from the family and rejection of their shared faith. Jonah wondered why Greg didn't take a stand and say something directly to their sister before she was completely lost. Instead of confronting Sarah, Greg had kept a close, warm relationship with her, and to a lesser extent, so had their parents.

After Jonah recounted his many concerns, he asked, "What can I actually do about this? I don't agree with what my family is doing, but what do I *do?*"

I felt for him. He seemed lost himself. His black-and-white, right-and-wrong idea of family life had turned many shades of gray. Absolutes had morphed into amorphous patterns that he couldn't recognize or understand. He didn't want to lose his family ties completely, so he asked if I could help mediate a session between him and his brother.

As I opened up the session, each brother spoke primarily to me about a long list of conflicts they wanted to address that evening. As we made our way through the lists, I noticed that they gradually started talking with each other rather than with me.

With the issues outlined before them, they brainstormed how they could still be true to their faith values while accepting that their sister had chosen a different life path. By the end of three hours together, I looked at both of them and asked, "How do you feel about your relationship with each other now?"

Jonah looked at Greg and answered first. "I feel really close to Greg. I understand him a lot better. I'm so glad that we took this time to talk through things. I still have a lot of questions for Mom, Dad, and Sarah, but I know that Greg and I both want things to work out with each other and our family."

Greg nodded in agreement and told his brother how much he loved him. "Jonah, we've got to keep talking. We can work through all these things."

I congratulated the two of them for their courage in opening up to each other and meeting with me. We eventually met for a second mediation with Jonah and his parents, which addressed other issues that had unsettled the family.

Through collaboratively sharing and listening to each other, all of the members of the family came up with a realistic plan for keeping each other close and thriving despite their differences.

When any of us use the Collaborative Approach in conflict, we put effort into effectively communicating so that we can come up with solutions that reflect the interests and needs of both sides. We take time to listen, talk through, brainstorm, and decide together how a problem should be resolved. When we collaborate, we demonstrate greater commitment to the relationship and an understanding that both sides have legitimate claims.

When and why do people use the Collaborating Approach?

While individuals have great capacity to effect change, many complex issues demand significant, ongoing collaboration involving various stakeholders. In truth, some problems take a literal village and more to resolve.

Soon after becoming mayor of San Francisco, Dianne Feinstein faced a major health crisis among her city's inhabitants. In the early 1980s, thousands of San Franciscans were dying of a mysterious immune disorder now known as AIDS, which had no known cure. While most leaders across the country were ignoring the issue, Mayor Feinstein got to work. She built cooperative networks to address the many challenges the city faced. In coordination with healthcare providers and engaged citizens across the city, Mayor Feinstein authorized the first locally funded AIDS services, creating the AIDS Task Force and the AIDS

Activity Office, which helped to coordinate and subsidize the city's response.

At a time when information sharing was critical for stemming the spread of the deadly disease, Mayor Feinstein organized a consortium of mayors across the country to exchange information between cities. Not only did she address AIDS healthcare issues, but she also worked with city officials to increase police presence in gay neighborhoods to prevent anti-gay violence. She also helped to pass legislation that prohibited discrimination against AIDS victims in housing, employment, medical services, and business.[16]

Mayor Feinstein could not have carried out any of these efforts on her own, but her initiative in choosing to *collaborate* rather than look the other way saved lives and encouraged her city's residents to take care of each other, even with limited resources. She chose collaboration, which inspired others to further work together to handle a crisis much larger than anyone initially expected.

While most of us will never be the mayor of a large city facing a dramatic health crisis, we do have roles and responsibilities that require cooperating with others to resolve issues beyond our solo capabilities. It's too early to tell, but as I write this book, I wonder which communities historians will see as the most collaborative and successful during the COVID-19 pandemic.

Collaboration is the last of the Five Conflict Approaches we can use in our most important stewardships, whether professional or personal. When we apply collaboration to our marriages, partnerships, and other close relationships, we will create more trust and respect.

Collaboration is the most underused conflict approach because it requires more skill and time than the other four approaches.

We often turn to collaboration either as a *first* step to demonstrate our goodwill or a reluctant *last* attempt at resolution after we have exhausted all the other (seemingly easier) methods. And sometimes we're *required* to participate in some form of collaboration if authorities, such as a school administrator, HR director, or a court, require it.

Some of us choose to collaborate as more of an initial step in demonstrating goodwill when first building a relationship with someone. Through collaboration, we try to show respect and consideration for others as a social investment of sorts. We hope to begin a positive pattern of interaction, so we show our openness to sharing and listening. Parents and teachers often use the Collaborating Approach to begin positive relationships with their children or students.

When we are in leadership roles, we usually seek collaboration because we want to set a precedent. We hope that by openly collaborating with others, we'll build trust and bolster our public image. Consider how many successful politicians survey their constituents to get a feel for what positions and policies are important to voters. They hold town meetings and other gatherings to talk through issues in order to demonstrate goodwill and understanding. And at the highest levels of government, private industry, and international relations, leaders meet in close, interpersonal settings to collaborate on issues that will become the public signals of their leadership. Sometimes the public approves of these collaborations, and at other times, they seem like a betrayal or sign of disloyalty.

In other situations, we collaborate because we don't understand the other person's or group's concerns well enough to make a hastier, less-informed decision. Because we're in the dark about our options, we check to see if others are willing to join together to find a solution that works for everyone. We're honestly curious and simply can't come up with solutions without other people's input.

Unfortunately, some of us turn to collaboration *only* when all other approaches have failed. After quicker, easier methods like avoiding or compromising don't come through for us, we bring a lot of added baggage—escalated emotion, skepticism about the other parties' motives, and just sheer conflict *fatigue*—to the table. We're sick of dealing with the things that won't seem to go away despite all of our wishful thinking. We finally confront a conflict with a Collaborating Approach because it's our last-ditch option.

Reluctant collaboration also happens when we're put in situations where we're "forced" by those in authority to collaborate with others in group projects at school or on work teams. In these cases, the outcomes are much less satisfying than when we choose to collaborate willingly. Trust cannot be manufactured or coerced. Forced collaboration fails to address the key ingredients of trust and vulnerability that provide the real power and energy for collaboration to work.

Rather than submitting reluctantly to collaborative approaches, why don't we choose this approach willingly when it seems appropriate? As parents, for example, we could try to collaborate more often with our children, especially our teenagers, who always want to second-guess our parental authority and competence.

Our voluntary and sincere efforts to collaborate with others helps build trust. These efforts convey empathy and respect while maintaining a balance between everyone's goals. Collaboration represents a more balanced approach than giving in to someone else's goals or demanding that another person or party give in to our wishes.

What are the benefits?

The Collaborating Approach puts us in a position to resolve more complex, ongoing problems and even change our attitudes and beliefs. Sometimes we are ready and willing to collaborate with each other to resolve difficult issues, but often we need guidance and encouragement to begin cooperating with each other.

In the film based on a true story, *Best of Enemies*, P.C. Ellis and Ann Atwater initially resisted collaborating with each other to help desegregate schools in Durham, North Carolina. In 1971, the City of Durham's chapter of the AFL-CIO brought in community leaders to hold a 10-day public meeting, or charrette, to settle ongoing issues with the Durham schools. As a civil rights activist, Ann Atwater was deeply skeptical about working with her co-chair, C.P. Ellis, who was the local Ku Klux Klan (KKK) president.

Atwater and Ellis were both interested in representing their communities in the public meetings. After initially refusing to even sit down with Ann to share a meal, C.P. Ellis gradually began interacting with Ann on a personal level. This led to him overcoming his racist views. Talking about his transformative experience, he shared:

> *I haven't been the same since I left that school program. All of this drastically changed my life...I mean, my thinking. How in the hell does people get so screwed up mentally? They [racists and segregationists] don't have any evidence to some of the things they do and some of the opinions they make.*

Ann later related how the collaborative public meeting process helped both her and Ellis shed their preconceptions about each other to begin cooperating for the good of the kids:

It wasn't until way down in the meeting, about the last week of it, is when the children talked to us and got us together sayin' that they wanted to go to school with each other and then we looked at each other like fools. We'd been arguing about the wrong thing and hadn't been doing anything to make the school system be better. That's when me and him started getting together...He decided that I wasn't as bad. He said, 'You ain't as bad as I thought you was.' And he started talkin' to me, and we started talking' back [and forth]. We went in the office and cried because we [had been] doing things the wrong way just because one was black and one was white.[17]

Your attempts at collaborating may not be documented in a film or have as dramatic of an outcome. But my guess is that, like Ann and C.P., your life will be greatly improved by focusing on the Collaborating Approach in a few key relationships that warrant your investment of time, energy, and effort.

When we see the ideal conditions for collaboration, we're wise if we focus on using the Collaborating Approach in our most important relationships. This approach demands interaction with people with great communication skills, a commitment to the relationship, and a certain level of trust. The benefits include:

- Collaboration helps us to build relationships with others and creates win-win outcomes.

- Collaboration expands our creativity and imagination and may result in innovative solutions.

- This approach may serve to balance power imbalances between different parties and groups.

- Our collaboration with others demonstrates respect and appreciation for them in a conflict.

All of our attempts to collaborate will not be received well or be successful. But by adding this important strategy to our toolbelt, we have greater chances for peace, especially in moments when we want to throw our hands up and say it's too hard. What is definitely too hard is staying in a conflict—with others or within ourselves—indefinitely and without hope for a resolution.

What are the drawbacks?

In my late twenties, I was riding the Tech Boom wave of 1999-2000 when I learned how complicated things can be in big enterprises. I'd always thought that if you're working for the same organization, you're on the same team. I expected that team members would assume the best, be helpful, and avoid playing games with each other.

As an international manager for a tech company in Washington, D.C., I often mingled with influential people from government, non-profits, and private industry. Our company headquarters were in California, but I was able to network face-to-face with D.C. leaders to benefit my company and team members. Some of my networking contacts related directly to my own responsibilities, while others I passed on to managers based in California.

Excited to help my company and fellow employees, I forwarded an American Red Cross contact to a female executive in a related position in the company, assuming she'd be pleased to have some help with networking. We had never met in person, but I knew her responsibilities and the overlap between our job stewardships.

I soon learned that she didn't appreciate my efforts. Everything blew up in my face one day when my boss called to say that he had just had an emergency meeting with *four* female executives who were furious about what I had been doing.

My boss shared with me some of the nasty complaints about my "encroachment," and I was crushed and astonished. I thought I was doing the right thing by sharing contacts, but these women saw my actions as predatory. Rather than collaborative, they perceived me as competitive and selfish. I tried to understand why my coworkers would be so threatened. I also wondered if I could be true to myself and my values when working with people who assumed the worst about me.

I now see that while I thought I was collaborating, I had missed cultivating the *essential element* in collaborative relationships. I had not taken time to develop adequate *trust* so that they would understand and receive my attempts to help them as genuine. Without trust, we can find ourselves in situations where we attempt to show kindness and cooperation, but our efforts are perceived as competition or judgment.

Real collaboration demands that both parties experience trust and a baseline of goodwill with each other. Without that trust, collaboration will probably fail.

Despite the strong emphasis in our society on collaborating with others in school, work, community, and home settings, it's not always the best choice for resolving conflicts, and it can be misused. If we attempt to collaborate with others over insignificant issues or assume greater trust or investment in the relationship than really exists, we'll be disappointed. A lot of the drawbacks of collaboration hinge on our *overuse of the process* when other approaches would be sufficient to resolve the conflict at hand. Some of those drawbacks include:

- Collaboration is time-consuming.

- It is not always worth your effort for insignificant issues.

- Collaborating may expose others' lack of commitment to a relationship.

- To be effective in collaborating, you need a certain level of trust in each other's sincerity, which is not always possible.

- All parties in the conflict must have decent communication skills (for example, active listening, reframing, and constructive questioning).

The Collaboration Approach typically demands our best communication skills, and we may struggle or fail to reach any kind of understanding if the other parties can't match our skill and motivation in resolving the conflict. Some people may overtly resist attempts to collaborate, and others may simply lack the understanding and skill to respond positively.

Of course, I suggest that you give the other parties the benefit of the doubt when you attempt to collaborate, but you should remain consciously aware of the skills and faculties of the other party so that you don't put yourself in a vulnerable situation. Sometimes your efforts will open you up to undue criticism, shame, and a sense of betrayal if others cannot reciprocate your openness or ability to communicate.

Please, test the waters first before diving into wholescale collaborative efforts that require deep trust and some positive relationship history.

If you are especially wary, finding a mediator may be helpful. A neutral third party can assist in buffering less-desirable communication patterns and fostering greater understanding between parties who have struggled in the past. I like to think of mediators (even friends or family who serve in this role) as communication assistants or process advocates, rather than as judges or decision makers.

What happens when we overuse the Collaborating Approach?

Remember that collaboration takes time and always involves some level of trust in others. Sometimes, we jump at the chance to collaborate even when more caution might be a good idea. I did just that when I was 21 years old. I was on a study abroad trip and couldn't stop thinking about James, this fabulous artistic man. He knew I was interested in him and flirted with me—and unfortunately, with several other girls in our program, too.

For days, he had pestered me about wrapping up our study abroad trip in the Middle East with a trip to France—just the two of us. I wasn't sure about how sincere his romantic feelings for me were, so I thought maybe traveling through France together might be the right step to help him see me as a girlfriend. After all, he was the one asking me every day about making the trip to France. Why would he do that if he wasn't interested in something more?

James insisted that we share all of our money and make our plans together—a real joint venture. We stayed for free with my friends throughout the country. I was convinced that his interest in this adventure meant he loved me, and my "sacrifices" would pay off in a real relationship by the end, so I agreed to all his plans, including sharing my money. (I know what you're thinking. But remember, I was just 21, and thought I was in love.)

We stayed with family friends from southern France to Normandie, and in my eyes, we were "making progress" as a couple. We were also having fun! I was sure my wholehearted collaboration had helped him to figure out how much he loved me.

One June day as we were walking toward the Seine in Paris, I finally realized I had made a terrible mistake. In a carefree way I will never forget, he looked ahead of me at the flowing river and said, "Here I am in the city of love with no one to love."

I drew a deep breath in and inwardly cringed.

Like my pre-emptive leap to "collaborate" with James, I'm sure you've jumped the gun and overused collaboration (or used it too quickly). As a mediator, I still sometimes turn to deep listening and seeking clarification from the people I work with when they don't really need it because they've already moved on from a simple conflict.

When you overuse the Collaborating Approach, you waste everyone's time and energy on insignificant issues. If the other parties know that conflict resolution with you will be quick, efficient, and involve limited pain and effort, they might engage. Instead, they learn to avoid trying to resolve conflicts with you because they don't want to get that deeply involved. Use your social savvy to gauge other people's interest and ability to collaborate before you begin.

What happens when we underuse the Collaborating Approach?

As I write this in 2021, our society is bearing the brunt of underusing the Collaborating Approach in so many areas, including healthcare, climate change, the student debt crisis, the opioid epidemic, and the growing gap between rich and poor. Without collaborative solutions, these and many other problems will go unresolved and become ever trickier to tackle when we finally muster the courage to confront them.

In too many domains, our lack of collaboration has created winners and losers in society, when that dichotomy isn't helpful at all. Making *no choice* is still a choice, and it leads to outcomes that are usually undesirable and unsustainable over the long run.

America's immigration policy is one area of insufficient political collaboration in the 21st century. With Congress failing to build consensus among legislators, immigration policy has been left to executive orders by the president and decisions by the judiciary. Adding to the disfunction instead of constructively addressing the complexities of immigration, political parties focus on skewering and blaming each other for policy failures, with no clear plan in sight.

When a U.S. president of either party unilaterally uses executive orders, this tends to breed discontent and backlash in members of the party not in power. Most Americans expect Congress to create and revise overarching immigration policies with input from all sides. Instead, each president's executive orders change how immigrants are handled and what border policies are implemented, all while there are nearly a million back-logged immigration cases pending in US immigration courts. This has increased the volatility of immigration policies. It's not rocket science. We need comprehensive solutions beyond building or not building a wall, and those sorts of comprehensive solutions only happen through *collaboration.*

To encourage collaboration between the House and the Senate and between Democrats and Republicans, we should consider how much most Americans actually do agree on critical questions, including the need for secure immigration pathways. In a 2019 Gallup poll, 76% of Americans considered immigration to be a good thing for the United States, with 81% supporting a pathway to citizenship for undocumented immigrants if they meet certain requirements. Bolstering these statistics are results from a 2016 Gallup poll among Republicans that saw a 76% support for a path to citizenship versus a 62% support for a border wall.[18]

The stakes are too high for society and for individuals when we choose not to collaborate with each other. Open wounds and a lack of progress on critical issues prevents our true peace and prosperity as a nation, but we can do better if we learn to collaborate personally and extend that learning to resolving conflicts as a society.

Undoubtedly, collaboration is the most underused of the Five Conflict Approaches because it requires the most skill, effort, energy, forethought, and respect for others as equal partners. Too often, we waste time and energy on first trying the "easier" approaches, which just aren't hearty enough to handle the tough, ongoing issues in our most important relationships. In these cases, we're already tired and annoyed by the conflict by the time we end up at collaboration. In a lot of cases, we would benefit by putting our initial investment in collaboration and build the trust, cooperation, and understanding that yields greater dividends in the future. This is especially true if we are collaborating with someone in an important ongoing relationship.

What are the ideal conditions for using the Collaborating Approach?

Rather than giving our hearts away before we know our love will be reciprocated or demanding that our kids obey our every word with no discussion, we should all seek sweet spots for collaboration and be willing to share with each other what we truly need. We should also spend time learning what the other person needs.

When I returned to the working world after my fifth child entered preschool in 2018, I wondered how I was going to balance work and family life. I had been hired to work 17.5 hours per week, which seemed manageable. But would my boss demand that I come in during inconvenient hours? Would I still be able to take my kids to school and walk the dog? I was willing to compromise my routine to make a good impression, but just how much would I need to give up?

During my first staff meeting, I sat huddled in a small office with my boss and a student worker to discuss how we were all going to work with each other in this new situation. I was replacing a full-time employee, so there would have to be adjustments.

"So, we haven't talked about our office hours yet. When should I be coming in?" I had hesitated to ask, but was more anxious about that question than anything else.

My boss looked up and simply asked, "What time do you think could work for you?"

I diverted the question back to him and Tim, the student worker, asking what their time constraints were. Tim shared his class schedule and my boss laid out his faculty responsibilities, and I started to see possibilities to create real balance in my life. I knew there would be sacrifices, but decided to share some of my family responsibilities instead of hiding them, as I had planned, to see if we could work around them.

"I've actually got kids in two different elementary schools and a dog to walk each morning."

Tim listened and suggested something even better than I had expected—a four-day work week with hours between

10 and 2 p.m. that would allow me to meet my family responsibilities easily. *Was this for real?*

I had gone into my first staff meeting in years thinking that I had to make all the sacrifices and accommodate my new coworkers with all that they wanted. Instead, we all contributed to a discussion sharing our needs and ideas. In the end, everyone got what they wanted and needed without making any real concessions. We just had to have a thorough enough discussion and review all the possibilities to know what could work for each person on the team.

When used in the right situations with people who trust each other, collaboration may strengthen and build our relationships and help us resolve seemingly incompatible differences. We're investing our time and effort to seek solutions that reflect the needs and wants of all people involved. We'll be most successful collaborating with others in conflicts with the following ideal conditions:

1. *Power is reasonably balanced between the parties.*

Rather than assume power over others, when you collaborate, you create patterns of shared power by openly discussing issues, providing growth opportunities, and brainstorming together.

2. *Both parties value the long-term relationship.*

When you collaborate with others, you demonstrate that you're thinking about your relationship down the road. From your first interactions, you can demonstrate this commitment and level of trust.

3. *Both parties display cooperative behaviors.*

You can begin a positive back and forth that leads to collaboration by encouraging others to share their thoughts and use their full talents. Rather than using your power to make people do what you want, you can thoughtfully explore the potential for reciprocity.

4. *There is sufficient time and energy to create a win-win solution that satisfies both sides.*

You benefit from setting aside more time than usual when you plan to collaborate. You should set aside time to prepare for the collaboration. You're usually investing in both resolving a conflict and bettering or maintaining an important relationship.

Rather than reject the opportunity to collaborate because you're intimidated by direct confrontation and deep conversation about conflict issues, consider how collaboration may wipe out a myriad of smaller conflicts at the same time. With an improved relationship, some of the small conflicts will disappear; you will be able to focus on the most important issues at hand.

In most conflict situations, you can either choose to invest time and effort for resolution upfront, or you can wait until the conflict has escalated and intensified and deal with it later. In Western society, we seem to avoid the preventive measures of collaboration and wait until the situation is unbearable before we choose to act. This can lead us to act aggressively. How much better would our lives be if we chose to set up regular collaborative processes like family meetings, regular couples getaways, and paid work retreats to invest in relationships that really matter to us? We ease the discomfort and difficulty of collaboration when we incorporate it into the key decision-making relationships of our lives, whether at home, work, or out in the community.

Questions for Reflection

1. When do I collaborate with others to resolve conflict?

2. What has been my experience with collaborating?

3. How effective am I at collaborating?

4. Whom do I collaborate with well? Why?

5. Whom do I have difficulty collaborating with? Why?

THE COLLABORATING APPROACH:

THINGS TO REMEMBER

In conflict resolution based on collaborating, you put effort into effectively communicating with the other party to try to come up with solutions that reflect all or most of the interests and needs of both sides.

When and why you may use the Collaborating Approach:

- You may want to show respect and consideration to others in the conflict.
- You may not understand the other person's or group's concerns well enough to make a hastier, less-informed decision.
- You may want to set a precedent of discussion and collaboration, which will serve to build trust not only with the other party, but also as part of your public image.
- You may finally turn to collaboration after other quicker, easier methods, such as avoiding or compromising, fail to resolve the conflict.
- You might even be "forced" to collaborate in situations like group projects at school or work teams.

Benefits:

- Collaborative approaches help you build relationships with others and create win-win outcomes.

- You may learn to balance power differentials between parties and groups.
- Collaboration will demonstrate respect and appreciation for others in the conflict.
- You might expand your creativity, resulting in innovative solutions.

Drawbacks:

- This approach may be time consuming and not worth the effort, especially for insignificant issues.
- Collaborating may expose others' lack of commitment to a relationship.
- You need a certain level of trust in each other's sincerity to make collaborating effective.
- All parties in the conflict must have decent communication skills, including active listening, reframing, and constructive questioning.

Don't overuse the Collaborating Approach:

- Sometimes collaboration can become tedious, wasteful, and misguided if overused.
- Others may learn to avoid trying to resolve conflicts with you because they don't have the time or energy for collaboration.
- You may miss out on resolving less important conflicts that others would willingly resolve using simpler, less time-consuming methods.

Don't underuse the Collaborating Approach:

- Collaborating is the most underused of the Five Conflict Approaches because it requires greater skill, effort, energy, and forethought.
- You may waste time, effort, and energy trying the other "easier" approaches, which are not hearty enough to handle tough, ongoing issues in our important relationships.
- You may benefit from putting initial investment into collaborating to build the trust, cooperation, and understanding that yields greater dividends in the future.
- Instead of waiting for the conflict to escalate and explode, take a crack at a greater investment, which involves some risk, especially your own vulnerability.
- You can ease the discomfort and difficulty of collaboration when you incorporate it into the key decision-making relationships of your life, whether at home, work, or out in the community.

Ideal Conditions for the Collaborating Approach:

1. Power is reasonably balanced between the people in the conflict.
2. You value the long-term relationship.
3. You display cooperative behaviors.
4. You have sufficient time and energy to create a win-win solution that satisfies everyone.

Chapter 7

Becoming Conflict Fluent

One Conflict at a Time

I look calmly but directly into Thomas and Sherry's eyes as I explain the conditions of their newly hatched plan.

"Do you both agree not to talk about divorce or marriage right now? Instead, we're going to try an experiment to see if you can learn to talk with each other without pain and misunderstanding. I don't know the future of your relationship, but we're going to see if we can create a new, tiny positive pattern based on your ideas."

After hours of back and forth, I am completely surprised that these two have decided to craft a joint anger management agreement to strengthen their trust with each other. The contract was their idea, not mine! For years, these two had struggled because Thomas needed to be heard through to the end of his thoughts while Sherry craved closure and support rather than intellectual probing.

During our second mediation session, both parties raised their voices, interrupted each other, and even cried in frustration. In short, it didn't look promising from my perspective. But I marveled at how I had gently called Thomas out on his competitive efforts to convince Sherry that she needed to stay married to him. His efforts to try to control the couple's narrative and emotionally force her to come back to him were backfiring, even during our session.

Instead of avoiding the topic of Thomas's ineffective competitive approach, I brought it up calmly and clearly. "Thomas, will you repeat back what you hear Sherry saying to you without any evaluation or judgment?"

Thomas began paraphrasing Sherry's thoughts but then fell back into complaining about her inflexibility. "She just cuts off all communication. She has no patience."

I jumped in again: "Thomas, will you please just repeat back what you heard Sherry say and check in with her to see if you have captured her thoughts correctly?"

I'm surprised that Thomas isn't offended by my directive. Instead, he tries again and manages to get Sherry's confirmation that he has heard her correctly. Thomas' simple gesture to understand without trying to control her has an immediate effect on Sherry. I can see in her face that she feels differently about Thomas when he isn't criticizing her for what she has said. Thomas has just demonstrated that he is not only willing but able to hear her without trying to change her—even if just for that brief moment.

Thomas and Sherry still have a long way to go in meeting each other's needs, but they are changing longstanding patterns that have hurt both of them for years. Despite my initial skepticism about their ability to get along, I am a witness that change is possible. With guidance, some trial and error (and occasional refereeing), both Sherry and Thomas began communicating without constantly inflicting pain on each other before my eyes.

Like learning any foreign language, it's impossible to become conflict fluent overnight. Improving how you resolve conflict and find peace will take time. But you *can* change one conflict at a time, making a positive impact on your life and the lives of those around you right away. Every day, you have opportunities to test out the Five Conflict Approaches and learn how to apply them more successfully.

We start with self-reflection. This is the first step in expanding our approaches to conflict beyond one or two preferred approaches, because we know our motivations and full histories.

What are my basic go-to strategies in conflict and what usually results? When my former boss called me a pleaser or an accommodator, I knew that something felt wrong about her label of my overall personality and approach. In my mind, I thought, "I'm more than that. I can stand up for things I believe in without being cowed into submission by a stronger voice or personality." By learning about the approaches, I got motivated to understand myself better and respond more effectively the next time.

Most of the time, we know we need to change, but we protect our egos and focus on trying to get others around us to change. We think *they* are the ones who are flawed and fueling the conflicts we face.

As Dr. Marshall Rosenberg suggested in *Nonviolent Communication*, we have four basic options for responding to negative messages we receive. We can (1) blame ourselves, (2) blame others, (3) sense our own feelings and needs, and (4) sense others' feelings and needs.[19] Each of these options leads to different outcomes.

From experience, we know that blaming ourselves or others for the conflicts we face does not lead us toward more resolution or peace. Rather than stew on blame, we can focus our energies on the second two options that point us toward learning to sense our own feelings and needs and helping others to sense their own feelings and needs. We are never without options. Even if it is difficult and requires great effort, we can be strategic in choosing how to respond with one of the Five Conflict Approaches.

When we become more self-aware and strategic in how we think through our conflicts, we begin to see and experience the "grays," or the "nuances," in our experiences. Many of our conflicts are multifaceted and involve rights and wrongs on both sides. Our conflicts are not usually black and white, with only one possible "right" outcome. As we mature and begin to see the nuances in our relationships, we recognize our need for expanded conflict resolution skills.

After recognizing your need for more adaptable and applicable approaches to conflict, take a deep breath and ask yourself: Do I understand how to avoid, accommodate, compromise, compete, and collaborate effectively?

With the basics of the five general approaches in mind, you can then choose a real-life situation and try one out. Rather than saying yes to a request for a favor, you might actually share that you're too busy right now. Or instead of avoiding a talk about a raise with your boss, you might role play the conversation with your spouse or friend, so that you don't freeze in the moment of opportunity. You can pick specific situations in which to try out new approaches and use trial-and-error. Those trials may involve some bumps and bruises, but that's how you learn.

We are all going to fail occasionally, and sometimes you'll crash and burn with your conflict resolution attempts. But you have every reason to hope that you will improve over time as you consciously apply the Five Conflict Approaches. You can harness your failures, dust yourself off, and get up again with increased understanding. Rather than remaining stagnant and not getting what you want out of life, you can continue searching for better answers and ways to respond to complex situations.

Naturally, you should plan for some discomfort and awkwardness as you adapt your natural conflict styles to new situations and strategies. When you have a small success in trying a new approach, you might consider expanding that approach on a larger scale in your life. You can review your efforts and make tweaks as needed. You might even ask a trusted friend or mentor for feedback about your attempts to resolve a conflict so that you can understand yourself better from another perspective.

Undoubtedly, changing your approaches to conflict will take time and effort. Anything really good and lasting takes work. But the possible rewards are endless. In successfully using avoiding and accommodating, you will prevent unnecessary conflict and empower others to live more peacefully themselves. Compromise provides quick solutions and mutual respect while competition will enable you to back up your important values and goals. In more complicated situations or relationships, collaboration fosters authentic connection and understanding. With these approaches, the real possibilities for conflict resolution become much more open and even unlimited in terms of improved chances for peace, harmony, and creating the life you desire.

Try practicing new approaches today. You will find much greater growth and improvement in your relationships when you are willing to try something new. Remember, successes *and* failures are absolutely critical for learning and growth, especially in conflict resolution. Your positive and negative experiences provide the contrast that allows you to truly see yourself and others.

With more time and experience, you will see how constructive conflict resolution actually creates greater and deeper connection with the people you value, connection not possible without the intimate interaction and sharing that comes with conflict.

APPENDIX

Literature Recommendations for

General Conflict Resolution Principles

Morton Deutsch, Peter T. Coleman, and Eric C. Marcus, eds. (2014). *The Handbook of Conflict Resolution: Theory and Practice.* This updated anthology provides a sweeping overview of conflict studies topics from academics while suggesting practical applications for implementation.

Roger Fisher and William Ury. (2011). *Getting to Yes: Negotiating Agreement without Giving In.* This business negotiation classic lays out the fundamentals of facilitative negotiation that underscores all facilitative mediation processes.

Marshall Rosenberg. (2003). *Nonviolent Communication: A Language for Life.* Dr. Rosenberg developed a four-step process for making requests based on observations, expression of feelings and needs, and a nonthreatening request.

Mental Health Resources

Mental health challenges are real and can be treated in a variety of ways. Please do not delay getting the help you and others need. Below, I suggest a small handful of book and app options to help you and others manage mental health challenges such as depression, anxiety, and addiction. While you have many options, I am pointing you to resources from healthline.com and goodrx.com due to the breadth and variety of the options they suggest.

Healthline.com staff recommended the following 15 books as the "Best Mental Health Books of 2021." Please visit healthline.com for more information.

- Best for people battling trauma: *The Body Keeps the Score*
- Best for science lovers: *Change Your Brain, Change Your Life*
- Best for anxiety: *Hope and Help for Your Nerves: End Anxiety Now*
- Best for recovery from addiction: *Recovery: Freedom from Our Addictions*
- Best for women survivors of relationship abuse: *Healing the Trauma of Abuse: A Women's Workbook*
- Best for understanding a therapist's perspective: *Maybe You Should Talk to Someone*
- Best for overcoming codependency: *Codependent No More*
- Best for battling burnout: *Burnout: The Secret to Unlocking the Stress Cycle*

- Best for healing from emotional pain: *Emotional First Aid*
- Best for understanding family trauma: *It Didn't Start with You: How Inherited Family Trauma Shapes Who We Are and How to End the Cycle*
- Best for self-awareness: *The Four Agreements: A Practical Guide to Personal Freedom*
- Best for navigating relationships: *Attached: The New Science of Adult Attachment and How It Can Help You Find—and Keep—Love*
- Best for highly sensitive people: *The Highly Sensitive Person: How to Thrive When the World Overwhelms You*
- Best for practicing self-love: *Loving Bravely*
- Best for finding order in life: *7 Habits of Highly Effective People*

While new apps are being created all the time, Healthline.com and goodrx.com have some current recommendations for helping with anxiety, depression, and substance abuse.

Healthline.com Best Apps for Anxiety

- Best anxiety app for meditation: Calm
- Best anxiety app for adult coloring: Colorfy
- Best guided anxiety app: Dare
- Best anxiety app for sleep: Nature Sounds Relax and Sleep
- Best meditation app geared toward people of color: Shine
- Best anxiety app for breathing techniques: Breathwrk
- Best anxiety app game: AntiStress Anxiety Relief Game
- Best anxiety app for hypnosis: Anxiety Relief Hypnosis
- Best anxiety app for journaling: Moodnotes

Healthline.com Best Apps for Depression

- Moodpath
- TalkLife
- Daylio Journal
- Youper
- What's Up?
- Sanvello
- Happify
- Relieve Depression Hypnosis
- CBT Tools for Healthy Living

Goodrx.com Best Apps for Managing Substance Use, Triggers, and Cravings

- Best overall recovery app: Pear reSET-O
- Best app for tracking sobriety: I Am Sober
- Best recovery app for finding treatment: SoberWorx
- Best recovery content app: Recovery Today Magazine
- Best recovery social networking app: Sober Grid
- Best recovery app to build good habits: Quitzilla
- Best recovery app to manage cravings and prevent relapse: SoberTool
- Best 12-step app: 12 Steps AA Companion App
- Best dual-diagnosis app: PTSD Coach

Conflict Style Assessments

If you are interested in learning more about your conflict styles, there are many free assessments available online. When participating in any survey about your personal behavior, assume that when you answer fewer questions, the results will be less detailed and provide fewer insights into your true patterns of behavior. However, if you are willing to pay for the assessment, the standard measurement for conflict style remains the fee-based assessment created by conflict theorists Kenneth W. Thomas and Ralph H. Kilmann. Their conflict styles assessment is known as the Thomas-Kilmann Conflict Mode Instrument (TKI).

Please remember that these are only tools to *suggest* your conflict styles tendencies. As I have explained throughout the book, I believe our styles are changeable. We may rely on one or two more cooperative approaches in one social situation, only to switch things up with more competitive behavior in a different circumstance. As human beings, we are dynamic and adaptable despite negative beliefs about our potential that we may have internalized over the years.

Finally, given our potential to adapt and switch our conflict styles depending on the social situation, please keep a particular situation or relationship in mind when you take any of the given assessments or quizzes. With specific conditions in mind, you are more likely to gain a focused and helpful insight into your patterns of conflict resolution behavior.

Free Web-based Conflict Style Assessments/Quizzes

United States Institute of Peace: Conflict Styles Assessment
https://www.usip.org/public-education/students/conflict-styles-assessment

University of Colorado-Boulder Conflict Style Quiz:
https://www.colorado.edu/today/2020/01/30/quiz-find-out-your-conflict-style

McGraw Hill Canada: Conflict Styles Assessment:
https://tools.mheducation.ca/college/mcshane4/student/olc/4obm_sa_13.html

The Blake Group: Conflict Management Styles Assessment
http://www.blake-group.com/sites/default/files/assessments/Conflict_Management_Styles_Assessment.pdf

Paid Conflict Styles Assessment by Conflict Theorists, Kenneth W. Thomas & Ralph H. Kilmann

The Assessment Site: The Thomas-Kilmann Instrument (TKI®)
https://theassessmentsite.com/product/the-thomas-kilmann-instrument-tki

Notes

[1] **Thomas and Kilmann**. While conflict theorists categorize conflict approaches in various ways, Dr. Kenneth W. Thomas and Dr. Ralph H. Kilmann emphasize that we have five general options for responding to conflict which include avoiding, accommodating, compromising, competing, and collaborating. Thomas and Kilmann have developed a conflict approach assessment tool that may be purchased by individuals at their website. Thomas, Kenneth W. and Ralph H. Kilmann, "Overview of the Thomas-Kilmann Conflict Mode Instrument (TKI)." Kilmanndiagnostics. com. http://www.kilmanndiagnostics.com/overview-thomas-kilmann-conflict-mode-instrument-tki (Accessed August 11, 2021).

[2] **The Five Love Languages**. Dr. Gary Chapman is a pastor, marriage counselor, and author who wrote this best-selling book. Chapman suggests that each person has a primary love language through which they receive and experience love. While each of the five love languages is considered important in a marriage relationship, Dr. Chapman emphasizes the importance of learning and focusing on your partner's main love language to enhance your intimacy and connection. Chapman, Gary D. (1992, reprinted 2015). *The Five Love Languages*. Northfield Publishing.

[3] **Conflict Fluency.** I first encountered the idea of conflict fluency in a book about intercultural conflict by Dr. Michelle LeBaron. Dr. LeBaron is a tenured professor at the University

of British Columbia (UBC) law faculty and director of the UBC Program on Dispute Resolution. LeBaron's book on bridging intercultural conflict influenced my thoughts about being skilled in each conflict situation like a linguist traveling through foreign lands. LeBaron, Michelle. (2003). *Bridging Cultural Conflicts: A New Approach for a Changing World*. San Francisco: Jossey-Bass.

[4] **Definition of Conflict from Thomas and Kilmann.** Thomas, Kenneth W. and Ralph H. Kilmann. "Overview of the Thomas-Kilmann Conflict Mode Instrument (TKI)." Kilmanndiagnostics.com. http://www.kilmanndiagnostics. com/overview-thomas-kilmann-conflict-mode-instrument-tki (Accessed August 11, 2021).

[5] **Dorothy Thompson.** Thompson was a newspaperwoman and writer. She was one of the few women working as radio broadcasters during the 1930s. She held significant influence in her day. "Dorothy Thompson Quotes" Goodreads, https://www.goodreads.com/quotes/77327-peace-is-not-the-absence-of-conflict-but-the-presence (Accessed August 13, 2021).

[6] **Understanding Conflict Origins.** Dr. Otomar J. Bartos (now deceased) and Dr. Paul Wehr, both former professors at the University of Colorado at Boulder, explore the three main sources of incompatible goals that fuel most conflict. These three sources include contested resources, incompatible roles, and incompatible values. See Bartos, Otomar J., and Paul Wehr. (2002). *Using Conflict Theory*. Cambridge University Press.

[7] **Negotiation: Communication for Diverse Settings.** Dr. Michael Spangle and Dr. Myra Isenhart, emeritus

professors and conflict resolution practitioners, explore the topic of negotiation from different angles, allowing the reader to understand negotiation broadly as well as within specific contexts. Spangle, Michael L. and Myra Warren Isenhart. (2003). *Negotiation: Communication for Diverse Settings.* Sage Publications, Inc.

[8] **Collaborative Approaches to Resolving Conflict.** Spangle and Isenhart identify sources of conflict beyond Bartos's and Wehr's three sources of goal incompatibility. They also explain that conflict may arise about what information counts, what procedures should be used for resolution, the degree of trust between parties, and particular communication styles. Michael L. Spangle and Myra Warren Isenhart. 2000. *Collaborative Approaches to Resolving Conflict.* Thousand Oaks: Sage Publications, Inc.

[9] **Differentiating Between Constructive and Destructive Conflict Patterns.** In the 2000 edition of *The Handbook of Conflict Resolution*, Morton Deutsch presents an interesting first chapter entitled, "Cooperation and Competition," comparing competitive and cooperative conflict management approaches. On pages 25–26, Deutsch lists the general outcomes for both competitive and cooperative approaches, which reflect the closing statements of chapter 2 in this book. Deutsch, Morton, "Cooperation and Competition," in Deutsch, Morton and Peter T. Coleman, eds. (2000). *The Handbook of Conflict Resolution*, pp. 21–40. Jossey-Bass.

[10] **Legalization of Marijuana in Colorado.** While marijuana has its medicinal purposes, there are social, physical, and emotional risks associated with its use and regulation. Rocky Mountain High Intensity Drug

Trafficking Area program (2019). The Legalization of Marijuana in Colorado: The Impact. *Missouri Medicine*, *116*(6), 450 and Schipani, Vanessa. "Unpacking Pot's Impact in Colorado." *FactCheck.org*, 19 August 2016. www.factcheck.org/2016/08/unpacking-pots-impact-in-colorado/. (Accessed August 23, 2021.)

[11] **Gun Control Measures in Australia.** "Firearms-Control Legislation and Policy: Australia." *Library of Congress: LAW*, Library of Congress. December 30, 2020. www.loc.gov/law/help/firearms-control/australia.php.

[12] **Romneycare in Massachusetts.** Goldberg, Martha. "Mitt Romney and Massachusetts Health Care: The Inside Back-story." WBUR.org, December 20, 2011. www.wbur.org/commonhealth/2011/12/20/mitt-romney-health-care; Robertson, Lori. "'RomneyCare' Facts and Falsehoods." FactCheck.org, March 25, 2011. www.factcheck.org/2011/03/romneycare-facts-and-falsehoods/

[13] **2015 Utah State Legislation to Address Religious and LGBT Rights.** Adams, Stuart J., "Cultivating Common Ground: Lessons from Utah for Living with Our Differences," in Eskridge, William N. and Robin Fretwell Wilson. (2018). *Religious Freedom, LGBT Rights and the Prospects for Common Ground.* University of Illinois College of Law Legal Studies Research Paper No. 19-07. 21 Pages Posted: 19 Feb 2019. Last revised: 20 Mar 2019. https://papers.ssrn.com/sol3/papers.cfm?abstract_id=3337029; "Explaining Religious Freedom and LGBT Rights." *Church of Jesus Christ of Latter-day Saints*. March 12, 2015. https://newsroom.churchofjesuschrist.org/article/explaining-religious-freedom-and-lgbt-rights. (Accessed August 23, 2021.)

[14] **Removal of Confederate Statues in the United States.** Waller, Alyson. "Charlottesville Can Remove Confederate Statues, High Court Rules." (April 1, 2021). *The New York Times.* www.nytimes.com/2021/04/01/us/charlottesville-confederate-statues.html (Accessed August 23, 2021); Moreno, Sabrina. "Richmond has removed the most Confederate symbols in the country since the killing of George Floyd. Here's how it happened." (September 4, 2020). *Richmond Times-Dispatch.* https://richmond.com/news/state-and-regional/richmond-has-removed-the-most-confederate-symbols-in-the-country-since-the-killing-of-george/article_ce8a0cfa-1621-5982-864c-bafcbad9e84b.html. (Accessed August 23, 2021).

[15] **Quaker Abolitionist Lucretia Mott.** Nugent, Patricia. "Lucretia Mott: 'The Lioness of the Convention.'" (March 2, 2015). *Ms. Magazine.* https://msmagazine.com/2015/03/02/lucretia-mott-the-lioness-of-the-convention/. (Accessed August 23, 2021). Wheeling, Kate. "What Made Lucretia Mott One of the Fiercest Opponents of Slavery and Sexism: Her humble Quaker upbringing taught her how to stand up for her beliefs." (July/August 2020). *Smithsonian Magazine.* https://www.smithsonianmag.com/smithsonian-institution/modesty-isnt-weakness-180975207/. (Accessed August 23, 2021).

[16] **Mayor Feinstein Addresses the AIDS Epidemic in the 1980's.** Allen, Karen. "The Provision of Care to People with AIDS in San Francisco; Past, Present, and Future." (June 1987). Senior Seminar, Environmental Sciences Group Major, University of California, Berkeley, student paper; Luce, John M. "A strange new disease in San Francisco: a brief history of the city and its response to the HIV/AIDS epidemic." *Annals of the American Thoracic Society*

10(2) (2013), pp. 143-7. doi:10.1513/AnnalsATS.201208-039PS; "Mayoralty of Dianne Feinstein." *Wikipedia.* https://en.wikipedia.org/wiki/Mayoralty_of_Dianne_Feinstein. (Accessed April 12, 2021); Roth, Rob. "Cleve Jones reflects on life in San Francisco during the 1980's AIDS crisis." KTVU Fox 2, (June 21, 2019). https://www.ktvu.com/news/cleve-jones-reflects-on-life-in-san-francisco-during-the-1980s-aids-crisis

[17] **Relationship of Ann Atwater and C.P. Ellis Captured in Film "Best of Enemies."** "Best of Enemies" (2019). *History vs. Hollywood.* https://www.historyvshollywood.com/reelfaces/best-of-enemies/ (Accessed 12 April 2021); Vaughan, Dawne Baumgartner. "'The Best of Enemies' tells a true story of NC History. What did the film get right?" (April 4, 2019). NewsandObserver.com, www.newsobserver.com/news/local/article228417999.html (Accessed August 23, 2021).

[18] **US Immigration Policy.** "Why Does the US Need Immigration Reform?" (May 2019). *Open Society Foundations.* https://www.opensocietyfoundations.org/explainers/why-does-us-need-immigration-reform; Felter, Claire, Danielle Renwick, and Amelia Cheatham. (June 23, 2020). "The U.S. Immigration Debate." *The Council on Foreign Relations.* www.cfr.org/backgrounder/us-immigration-debate-0. (Accessed August 23, 2021).

[19] **Responding to Negative Messages**. Marshall Rosenberg. (2003). *Nonviolent Communication: A Language for Life.* Dr. Rosenberg developed a four-step process for making requests based on observations, expression of feelings and needs, and a nonthreatening request.